COMPUTER ETHICS
A Guide for a New Age

COMPUTER ETHICS
A Guide for a New Age

Douglas W. Johnson

The Brethren Press
Elgin, Illinois

COMPUTER ETHICS: A Guide for a New Age

© 1984 by Douglas W. Johnson

The Brethren Press, 1451 Dundee Avenue, Elgin, IL 60120

Cover design by Vista III Design

Edited by Leslie R. Keylock

LIBRARY OF CONGRESS CATALOGING IN PUBLICATION DATA

Printed in the United States of America

This book is dedicated to two
professors whose teachings and example
have guided my ethical understanding of
life and society:
Murray H. Leiffer
and
Walter G. Muelder

CONTENTS

FOREWORD

Mankind's history has been marked by major turning points. The invention of the steam engine, for example, brought the Industrial Revolution and shifted the burden of labor from human backs to machines. In this century, the automobile and telephone have drastically influenced the way we live. Now comes the computer, which promises—or threatens—to impact our lives more quickly, more dramatically, than could have possibly been foreseen when the now ubiquitous machine was invented just four decades ago.

Hardly any aspect of our lives goes untouched by computers. Yet the public's relationship to computers is a fragile one. Part of the reason is that most people don't understand computers and what they can and cannot do. Other people resent the impersonal nature of computers. Still others have an outright fear of them. They see computers as devices that threaten to control them, rather than vice versa. Much of the reason for the public's uneasy relationship with computers comes from the suddenness with which they have entered our lives.

Yet the public will adapt to the changes the computer has introduced, just as it has adapted to the changes brought about by other revolutionary developments. As change comes, there will be an ever-growing need to assure people that computers are a force for good in society as a whole. The computer holds untold potential for humankind in education, medicine, science, the workplace, and countless other areas. But it threatens to widen the gap between the haves and the have-nots of the world. As one example, consider the long-range implications of elementary school students in a wealthy school district working daily with computers, while children in an inner-city school a few miles away are denied that opportunity because their school district can't afford the machines. Which group of students will be better prepared for the future that is certain to come?

In this book, Douglas Johnson addresses the issue of computer ethics, a vitally important yet perplexing subject that desperately needs to be addressed while the computer age is still in its infancy.

Walk into any computer store today, and you will see computers and computer accessories on display, along with software to run the computers, instruction books, and computer magazines. Yet one will not find any book, any reference material, that discusses the rights and wrongs of computer usage from an ethical position. There simply is no set of guidelines or rules—save one's own standard of conduct—to govern the use of the computer. (Can you imagine what kind of havoc we would have without traffic rules and regulations governing the use of automobiles?)

Stories frequently appear in the press telling of the way computer "hackers" have illegally gained entry to data bases of government units, corporations, and even patient records at hospitals. When caught, these people—mainly teen-agers—assert they meant no harm but were merely reacting to the challenge of demonstrating their mastery of computer and communications technology. These people would hardly consider picking the lock on a neighbor's door to gain access to the neighbor's house. But the computer, communications lines, and data bases are highly impersonal things—unlike a neighbor's house.

This is the challenge facing those concerned about computer ethics—raising the consciousness of the public so that the computer is not merely considered a cold, mechanical thing but something that affects all of us in a most personal way.

Ray Shaw, President
Dow Jones & Co., New York, N.Y.

PREFACE

It's a long way, conceptually and actually, from a one-room schoolhouse in rural Illinois to life in a computer-oriented society in the New York metropolitan area. Yet some of us have made that trek and others have made similar social and psychological journeys as they have matured into a computer-dependent society. While children in elementary schools may think computers are normal tools of learning, adults, especially those over fifty, know how difficult it is to trust a machine. The acceptance of computers by these adults is intellectual and often is accompanied by considerable skepticism.

Personal computers came into the home and work place like a tidal wave in the early 1980s. They have given even the most skeptical a new tool. In many instances the personal computer has unleased creativity that was stifled by the demands of work. We are discovering—inventing might be a better term—a new age. This will be governed by our relationships to and dependence on computers.

Every new age demands of its people rules for getting along in a new environment. The age of computer dependency brings requirements for adapting rules for living. This book is an effort to speed the discussion of how those rules and environments might look. The book applies the experience and teachings of others in a manner that can be useful in a computer age.

An author must address issues from a particular set of experience and learnings. Many have contributed wisdom, suggestions, and insights to what is contained in the following pages. I am grateful to the people who have been a part of groups and conversations and am hopeful they can see their contributions. I hasten to add that I am responsible for the content and interpretations of what they shared.

Douglas W. Johnson

Chapter 1

COMPUTERS EVERYWHERE

Computers are everywhere. There's one in the gas station down the street, one in the library, two dozen in the school two blocks away, ten in the school one block away, half a dozen in as many friends' homes. Large rooms are filled with computer apparatus in universities and large businesses.

For many of us the little machine sitting on our desk or table has brought home the computer age. Computers are everywhere, perhaps even in front of you as you read. Millions of Americans are already using them every day.

The computer promises to make as many changes in our lives as the family and business car did years ago. It revolutionized social and economic life in the early and middle years of this century. The high technology revolution promises to affect the way we live, shop, and work. It is a huge industry now, and its future potential is enormous.

The Wall Street Journal reported that by 1995 home owners would spend $11 billion a year on computer-based home information systems (April 14, 1983, page 1).

The Sunday Record, a northern New Jersey newspaper, reported on June 5, 1983, that every new home in a planned community near San Francisco, California, was being wired with two computer locations. In addition, the builders will allow the buyers to finance up to $3,500 of computer equipment as a part of the home's mortgage.

A *U. S. News and World Report* feature entitled "Behind the Shakeout in Personal Computers" on June 27, 1983, indicated that in 1982 the sales of personal computers totaled $6.0 billion, the 1983 estimate was $8.8 billion, and the 1987 estimate was $28.0 billion. It also reported that approximately 200 manufacturers were in the market place vying for those dollars.

Those little machines have touched everyone. Two small-town Midwesterners were discussing recent articles in their local newspaper.

"Computers! Computers! That's all anybody seems to talk about! I'm getting a little sick of all this noise about computers. What's so big about them? They've been around for a while. It isn't as if everybody was going out to buy one tomorrow."

"Well, I'm not sure about that. See that new car over there? It's got a computer in it. Something to do with gas feed and exhaust. And then there's Bob out north of town. He's got a computer that he uses to help mix the feed for his cows."

"You don't say! Bob? I'd never guess he'd know anything about a computer. When did he get it?"

The news stories and this conversation are clues as to how important computers are in our society. We don't live in an agricultural, industrial, service, or postindustrial society any longer. We are in a computer society. Much of our life is governed by what's on those small chips found in computers. (They really aren't chips so much as small plastic rectangles with wiring.)

Those chips tell more about people and machines than we would dare to believe. The data chips, which are read by electronic devices attached to a computer, are found in offices, cars, telephones, television sets, and just about every electronic appliance we have in our homes. An encoded chip is regarded as the ideal replacement for those metal "dog tags" soldiers have worn for so long. That little silicon chip is making us increasingly computer dependent.

The phrase "computer dependent" may sound ominous to many people. However, it simply describes a social condition, just as "agriculture dependent" denotes another kind of society. We live differently from earlier societies because we make use of the computer and they didn't. Being computer dependent is not bad in itself. It has its benefits. For example, relying on computers to store and read information easily and quickly allows us to carry more data about ourselves than we could have imagined a few years ago. A plastic computer card can contain the history of our illnesses, allergies, and treatments. If they are available to ambulance or emergency room personnel, these bits of information can even save our lives.

Living in a computer society not only makes demands on us, it also benefits us. We must, however, know how to use the computer and understand the rudiments of how it can be controlled before it can be a useful servant. We will have to change the way we think and act. We will have to become conversant with the computer. There is a lot of emphasis now on helping people become "computer literate."

A brief article in *INC.* magazine for July, 1983, reported on a program at West Virginia University in Morgantown designed to teach three-year-olds how to use a computer. The professor in charge feels the computer is an excellent tool to teach children how to read and write. That's taking computer literacy seriously!

Take a walk into the junior high across the street from me. The most popular courses offered are the computer courses. There the students are signing up to learn how to use and program computers, including the personal computer. The emphasis in this community and in many others across the nation is on helping young people understand how to use a computer. Teachers and administrators realize that unless junior high students know how to use and program the computer, they will begin their adult lives at a disadvantage. We aren't, therefore, looking at a passing fad. Computers are here to stay.

Increased Creativity

A significant benefit of the proliferation of computers is the potential for increasing people's creativity. Since the computer is so fast, it allows individuals to put into its records thoughts and decisions as quickly as their fingers can move. The computer, as a tool, relieves people of much of the boredom of making tedious calculations. It lets actuarians, for example, concentrate on trends and find other data to influence decisions rather than spend their days working out tables on which to base projections. The potential for individual creativity is available because of the computer.

"One of the things I've discovered is how much more I can get done using a computer than I can with a typewriter and calculator," a friends said to me the other day.

"I know what you mean," I replied. "I type faster and am more accurate because it isn't hard to make corrections. I don't have to retype an entire page if I make a mistake on the last line. I can make one simple change, and the computer keeps everything else as it was."

In *The Word Processing Book*[1] Peter McWilliams describes the increase in speed and accuracy he experienced with he started using a computer. Not only did his writing improve, but he used his newly-purchased computer to help him do research as well. The computer improved his creativity and freed him from some of the more mechanical processes of writing.

A business friend, after purchasing a personal computer, found that he could improve his business because he had new capabilities. He could follow up customers by using personalized form letters that he typed on his computer. All he had to change each time was the name and address. In addition, his bookkeeping, inventory, and client lists became much more accurate because he didn't have to keep retyping them. He cut the amount of time he spent because he did not have to look them up on long forms. Instead, he used the computer to store, sort, and display the names, accounts, and history of his dealings with each customer. These improvements relieved him of certain kinds of worries and allowed him to concentrate on doing what he does best — selling.

These stories could be multiplied by the experiences of individuals in many rural areas in the nation as well. Keeping track of dairy farm feeding, milking, and calving; monitoring growth and production rates of varieties of grain; maintaining moisture levels at different temperatures in silos and storage bins; monitoring water levels in fields, and opening irrigation gates or turning on sprinklers; and a host of other chores are being controlled by personal computers. Each of these chores was once done by hand. The computer frees people to do other jobs, jobs that require human thought and reasoned decisions. In innumerable ways people are freed from monotonous, repetitive tasks that are essential but that can now be done by computers.

The computer creates a different kind of life pattern for individuals. They have far more opportunities to be creative.

Increased Capabilities

The increased use of computers has eliminated more drudgery than many people thought possible only a decade ago. For example, a student was asked to use a calculator to figure two pages of problems, each of which required a complex formula. It took him two days to complete the task.

Later, that same student was asked to put the problems through a computer. It took ten minutes!

He concluded that the two days he had used in tabulating the problems taught him patience, while the ten minutes of computer time had shown him a much more productive life pattern. Patience might be a virtue, but freedom from drudgery is much more appealing.

In industry today, robots controlled by computers do dangerous and boring jobs such as welding and removing toxic or dangerous wastes. In earlier times, such jobs went to the newest employees or those least liked by the employer. Now, people are freed from these kinds of tasks. Machines with replaceable parts are used instead of humans, whose parts are usually not substitutable.

The New York City bomb squad uses a robot controlled by an internal computer to remove suspected bombs. While industrial and police use of robots controlled by computers has not been perfected, the fact of their existence and use means that fewer people will be killed or maimed in our efforts to do dangerous jobs essential to an industrial society.

A similar change of dramatic proportions has occurred in business. A few years ago, the New York Stock Market considered the trading of fifty million shares in a single day to be unrealistic. Currently, a trading day in which fifty million shares change owners is considered to be slow. The future will increase that figure. The reason for these changes in perceptions has been the capability of computers. People with mechanical processors could not make the necessary changes in stock ownership to handle fifty million shares in a day. High speed computers not only make it possible, but they have changed the kinds of jobs needed. Now there are fewer transaction clerks, but the more creative tasks of research and trading have been enhanced. These changes have meant dislocation, but the result has been better use of people's talents and time.

It does not always follow that people actually make better use of their talents and time because of the computer, however. Doing something that is more productive generally demands discipline and often leads to the need to learn new skills. Many people prefer not to be bothered. But that's a human choice made possible by those little chips that are the backbone of a computer.

Misunderstanding

One church included a course on the computer in its adult education program. Forty people attended each week for a month. An older participant gave as his reason for attending, "I haven't the slightest idea about computers, and I want to learn about them. I don't want to have the wrong impression of what they are or can do."

The "community schools," adult education programs for community citizens, have in several areas during the past few years offered courses on becoming acquainted with the computer, computer programming, and advanced computer programming. The enrollment has been filled each time. The primary reason for the courses has been the desire of adults to learn about computers and what they can do for them. The emphasis of the courses has been on using personal computers in home and business. The instructors have been professionals who use small computers in their work.

In one adult discussion group the fear was raised time and again that computers would take over thinking for humans. The leader assured the group several times that thinking was a human activity. If computers gained that capacity, it would be because humans had so programmed them. In other words, the computer is a tool for people to use. While this allayed the fears of several participants, some clung to the notion that computers would take over the world. They feared "Big Brother" with an almost paranoiac delusion.

A business executive discussing computers for managers said, "Age seems to be a factor in using computers. Most of our people over fifty aren't interested in learning how to use them, whereas all of those under forty are eager to have their own. It's a generation thing. The younger group sees the computer as a tool, whereas the older group doesn't want to adapt to it."

Those who grew up in the punch card era were taught that the computer was a mysterious machine that could be used only by technicians who spoke its language. They saw it as a mystery box that could do many things very quickly. They also felt like those who learned of the accuracy of the 1952 presidential election projections and the debacle caused by the technicians who wouldn't believe the machine.[2] The machine proved correct, and the operators were wrong. The computer assumed a mysterious and nearly omniscient aura for people in the period that followed. They didn't know how it worked, but they knew that it was fast and more accurate than most of them.

The computer is not a black box that produces accurate information without assistance. Clearing up misunderstandings about its capabilities takes much of the time of beginning courses in computer science, especially for adults. They have problems viewing it as a machine controllable through words and electronic impulses. They prefer to hold to the notion that it is somehow superhuman. That myth produces fear and mistrust.

On the other hand, young people have perhaps too little fear and not enough mistrust.

Computer Dislocation

A workshop leader, immediately following an hour's presentation on what the computer is and can do, was talking to another leader. "One of the things I've noticed about these workshops is that people who have computers are almost irrational about them.

They aren't able to speak objectively about what computer systems, other than their own, can do. They are mystical about the powers of their computer."

"I've noticed the same thing," the other leader replied. "When I've spoken with families about the computer in their homes, I've also noticed that it can cause a great deal of tension in the family."

"How's that?"

"The computer operator—husband, wife, or child—gets hooked on the machine. He begins to discover something he can control. His energies are absorbed in creativity as it relates to the machine. In other families, games absorb days at a time."

"That's one way to cut out family entertainment! I'll bet it's even been the cause of some divorces."

"I'm not certain of that, but it has created a lot of dissatisfaction. The main criticism I've had is, 'He's always sitting in front of that computer. We can't get him to do anything else. It's disgusting!'"

A recent newspaper story indicated that one parent's way to punish his teenager was to deprive him of the use of his computer. That kind of deprivation begins to indicate the extent to which we have become addicted to the computer. When it becomes the primary focus of a person's attention, other aspects of life begin to suffer.

One man indicted the computer by pointing out that computer games had taken the risk out of life for some people. "Young people today don't take risks," he said. "They're afraid of risks. They would rather play video games. There the risks don't involve anything of themselves and when they lose, it doesn't affect them personally."

Such a statement suggests that computers can be allowed to short-circuit the developmental processes of young people. Traditionally, the teen years have been the time when experimenting and taking risks have been expected. If many teens are now focusing their risks on machines, they may be less able to deal with future problems that require thought and reasoning, rather than the agile manipulation of hands and eyes.

Another form of dislocation is social. It may be increased

divorce, separation of people from their workplace, or clocking people's productivity rather than dealing with them as people. Each of these developments has become a reality during the past couple of years. This may suggest the beginnings of serious social problems in the future.

It is easy to understand how a family can gradually grow apart. It happens when a parent or a child becomes completely absorbed in working with a computer. Since the computer can become almost as addictive as alcohol, reality can be what is seen on the computer screen. Gradually, personal connections with the family can be replaced by hook-ups with other computer buffs. Interaction with other people then occurs chiefly through computers, using the telephone lines. The spouse can be left out. Separation and divorce are then very real possiblilities.

Working with a computer at home has been the topic of several recent stories in newspapers and magazines and on television. One such article, in *The Record*, a northern New Jersey newspaper, described one company that specialized in home work on the computer (May 3, 1983). It indicated that the people who work at home like the set-up. They tend to be women who want to continue a career while children are growing up, or men who prefer to be at home rather than work in an office. One difficulty in such an arrangement, however, is the lack of association with fellow workers.

Work at home, the technological cottage industry Alvin Toffler describes in *The Third Wave*,[3] is adding income to many families. It can, however, also increase the stress they feel. A segment of an NBC "Monitor" program in mid-July, 1983, dealt with at-home computer jobs. Those interviewed for this program indicated that they received no benefits, other than salary, and were essentially doing piecework much as a seamstress does piecework. While the question of exploitation was not raised overtly, it was strongly hinted at. The program indirectly posed the question of whether working at home on the computer was a new version of the sweatshop so familiar to the New York garment industry.

A much more serious problem posed is the accuracy and time-keeping abilities of computers. The front page of the May 6, 1983,

Wall Street Journal reported on one company's use of the computer to monitor employee productivity. Computers measure each employee's production based on a time standard set for each task. This process is, in effect, the computerization of the scientific management theories developed by people like Frederick Taylor. With computers, time and motion engineers can actually employ the tactics suggested by these theories. The result is increased stress and employee recognition that everything other than work means less money.

The computer can be a boon to individuals and society, but it can also be a negative factor for families, individuals, and the society. With an increasing number of computers, especially small computers on managers' desks and in homes, serious attention needs to be directed to their proper use. Since the younger generation views them as a tool or even as a key to a successful future, it becomes important to think about how they can be used responsibly and not simply as a control mechanism. The computer must not be used to exploit people, even though it has that capability because of the data it has stored about most of us.

Ethics

A coordinator of computer courses in a school system was quoted as saying that the basic issue in computers is ethical. She was discussing the abilities of students to understand the computer. They knew about it, could use it well, and considered it an important part of their lives. The problem from her point of view, however, was that they were not limited by any moral rules against copying other people's programs, from keeping data that could be harmful to others, or from using the computer to gain access to the school's grading system. She felt it was time to develop a set of computer morals and to teach them. Those most needing such a code of ethics were people with computers in their homes or offices; indeed, all those who felt they had complete control over their computer and what went into it.

The Random House College Dictionary defines ethics as "the rules of conduct recognized in respect to a particular class of human actions." In this case, the rules of conduct pertain to the use of a computer in a computer-dependent society. We have lived with a basic morality that has evolved from an agricultural to an industrial to a service-oriented society. During the past decade, however, we have jumped from being a service-oriented society to a computer-dependent society. Unfortunately, an adequate morality for this new society has not yet evolved.

The ethical base for constructing a new morality is already present, however. Some of the rules are already contained in laws, such as the copyright laws. Consumer laws that protect buyers from shoddy merchandise and high pressure sales tactics are also in existence. Better Business Bureaus around the country have been watchdogs in customer and merchant relationships. Nevertheless, the emphasis of most of the laws has been on services and products about which people are informed. That often doesn't include the purchase, use, and service of computers in the home.

Everyone, for example, has been told over and over to beware of the used car salesman. He has a reputation for selling products that are without warranties and could end up costing hundreds or thousands of dollars more than the listed price. Not many consumers, however, are warned about computer sales people who know little or nothing about the products they sell and for which they have neither warranties nor service facilities to assist customers who happen to buy a defective product. Neither have many companies engaged in educational advertising to help a potential purchaser know what kind of computer package would be most useful for his or her home or business. The ethics developed around auto sales, limited though they are, have not been translated into helpful conduct codes for the high tech field of computers.

It's little wonder, then, that people become disillusioned with their computer purchases. They become frustrated with the lack of knowledge about or interest in their computers by those who sold them to them. For example, when I wanted to purchase a home computer, I went to four different stores that were advertising home computers. The advertisements said each store had employees who could explain and demonstrate the computer's use. Yet not one of the four stores I visited had an individual who knew more than how to turn the machine on. It immediately became apparent that the stores could provide no back-up or service to the products they sold.

Many other computer owners could tell similar stories or relate experiences about trying to find a technician to answer a simple question about their system or a particular type of software. The industry has grown so quickly that many of the dealers and software developers have had no time to develop ways to help us when we run into problems. Laws may be available but until they are applied to home and business computers, relief is not in sight.

Take the copyright law as an illustration of this point. Problems occur in enforcing the copyright statute when computers are in homes and on the desks of thousands and millions of people. How is it possible to monitor the law and arrest and punish offenders when there are so many? Does the government have the right to invade homes to see if the program an individual is using has been stolen because it has been copied from a friend? We must develop a code that allows monitoring to occur among friends. Codes of conduct are more important than laws when so many individuals are involved. At issue is getting people to accept general rules of conduct regarding other people's property and rights when it is so easy to pirate programs and steal ideas.

Invasion-of-privacy laws have been enacted that limit the ability of government and business to gather data on individuals. The extension of those laws to home and business or managerial computer operators has not yet been understood as important or feasible. Ethics is essential to a computer-based society, not because the phenomenon of computers is new, but because the number of individuals who use them has increased manyfold.

The development of a body of ethics related to computers has not been of major concern, although the issue of privacy of information and the copyright laws has received considerable attention. Part of the problem in developing an ethic is that professional computer associations have codes of conduct that govern those in charge of "mainframe" or large computer configurations. They have not extended those codes to managers who now have computers for personal use, nor to other nonprofessionals.

Another part of the problem is that computer use has become widespread only since the early 1980s with the advent of the inexpensive home and business computers. The new computer operators are not professionals in the same sense as the people who are in charge of large computer installations.

Home and business computer users are individuals who have found a new way to do their work and might easily discover uses for computers that could injure others. Society cannot await a task force to investigate the need for ethics in a computer era. Such an ethic must be developed immediately, and by those who have most to gain by the surge of computer sales. Yet they do not appear to be overly concerned with the issue.

A professional computer programmer with whom I discussed the computer and ethics said, "The computer is amoral. It's the operators who are the problems. In our business, we know who they are and they are soon out of jobs."

A participant in a workshop on computers and privacy[4] suggested that the major ethical dilemma in computer use in the future may not be "Big Brother" but the person next door or in the manager's office down the hall who has accumulated data about one's habits through observation and conversation. The development of ethical standards must address such individuals and allow for the redress of grievances against them, as well as against the major corporations with large computers that contain data about them and their finances.

Humane Transition

Computers are everywhere. Young people know how to use them. Private individuals in the community use them for anything they want. Computer manufacturers have not taken seriously the ethical problems the use of small computers by managers or people at home creates. Only a few manufacturers have created a competent, well-trained network of dealers. The public has received some instruction in what to look for, but the sales people in many computer stores are less than helpful to any but the most inexperienced computer user.

The computer industry has publicly discussed individual privacy and copyright laws as they relate to business and government. But for those with computers in their homes or on their desks, none of the ethical issues relating to computer use has been discussed.

Yet, as Toffler points out,[5] society is becoming more individualized and privatized. Such a movement must be accompanied by rules of conduct and behavior that allow individuals to use their computers and at the same time safeguard the rights of others. A responsible society must be composed of responsible individuals. Developing an ethic for a computer society is not a luxury but a necessity for those of us now in that society.

In spite of our historic emphasis on individual freedom, we must realize that we also have a responsibility toward others. It may require us to limit our eagerness to protect our own rights to some extent. A society is designed to ensure the rights of all of its citizens, not the rights of a privileged few. That is a primary reason for the suggestion that we must work together to establish a new ethic for this computer society.

Chapter 2

PUTTING PERSONAL DATA
IN YOUR COMPUTER

"What I would really like to do is to go some place where no one knows me and live without any pressures. I could live as an anonymous person," one computer owner said to another.

"There are days when that sounds good, I have to agree. Unfortunately, with all the data that are stored about me in various computers around the country, I'm certain it wouldn't be long before somebody found me," the other replied.

"Yeah, but just think. You might get away with it for a year, or two, or even four. That might make it worthwhile."

"Not when you know they're going to find you. It would be like living on pins and needles all the time. If it wasn't for those data banks, maybe it might be possible."

This conversation was between two people who knew their personal data were stored in computers in banks, in credit unions, with the government, and in credit card financial centers. They knew that eventually they could be traced through the data in those files. What makes the fantasy they were describing possible is the missing data. There usually isn't information about a person's personal characteristics or habits in computers. The lack of that kind of information makes it possible for many people to "get lost" for days, months, and even years. Computers can't find us because they hold only part of our files—yet!

People disappear every day in this nation. They just walk away from their homes, jobs, and families. One of the ways authorities cope with this problem, espcially when teen-agers are involved, is by developing a national computer file in which descriptions, names, and identifying characteristics of teens and sub-teens who run away from home are contained. The intent of this project is to establish a computer net through which fewer and fewer people, especially teen-agers, can drop out of touch with their families.

Such a network will give parents and families hope when a child or family member runs away. Without a computer net, runaways are difficult, nearly impossible, to locate. A more complete personal data file in a nationwide computer net could help the police trace people.

Such personal data, even if it is limited, is a good thing for most of us to have in computers. Such a computer file would allow us the advantage of living in a credit economy, give us automatic banking, provide job seekers the opportunity to get their names out to potential employers, and in general make life easier and more pleasant.

This is not to overlook the problems each of us has encountered because a computer operator had a bad day and carelessly entered incorrect information about us. In spite of these discomforts, computers contain personal information that makes life easier for all of us. If it becomes a choice of working with someone to clear up a computer mistake or not having data available in the computer at all when we need it, most of us would opt for straightening out the mistake.

Immediate Clearances

One of the most obvious benefits to having personal data in computers is the clearances we receive when we want to cash a check or make a purchase using a personal check. These clearances are so much simpler than we experienced a few years ago. Then, it seemed, we had to bring everything but our birth certificate as verification in order to make a purchase. Those who remember when computers were not used to clear checks can still recall the cages in which hard working persons were located whose sole task was to look up on typed lists our bank's verification of our financial worthiness. This may be an inaccurate memory on my part, but it comes to mind every time I have a long wait at a check-out counter or at a cashier's station in a department store.

While personal check clearance has improved greatly, an even more fantastic change has come in another part of our personal banking. Many of us carry a plastic card issued by a bank that we can use to make deposits, withdraw cash and transfer funds in our accounts through an automatic teller machine connected by computer to our bank. The card contains information about us that the computer verifies before it grants us access to our accounts and the funds we have available. Using this card makes banking much more convenient. No longer do we have to live according to the bank's schedule! Our transactions can be done on our own schedule even if that's midnight on a weekend! That's a revolution for most of us.

Another place we notice the use of personal data in computers is in the grocery store. Many grocery stores, especially those in urban areas, issue people identification cards that can be used when they want to pay for their purchases with a check. The customer can purchase groceries and supplies, take them to the check-out counter, and present the card to the cashier, who then enters the number on the card into the computerized cash register. The computer verifies with a bank list that the customer's account has money enough to pay for the check. This process allows a customer's personal check to be immediately approved or rejected.

Purchasing by credit card is an important way for many people to buy products and services. Credit cards are used frequently because it is so easy to secure credit clearance either through a computer terminal at the cash register or by the use of a telephone call. The computer somewhere contains financial data about us that assures the seller that what we purchase will be paid for.

It is obvious from these illustrations that computers are becoming increasingly essential to us in most of our financial activities. In fact, in some places it is nearly impossible to pay for purchases in cash without having a credit card available to verify who we are and that the money we carry was not stolen. Immediate clearances are so routine we now take them for granted. It's human nature to complain, or at least so it seems, because we are leery of the fact that our personal information is stored in computers. Take away that data and those computers, and we would complain more loudly because we would be so inconvenienced!

Personnel Placement

All those forms we complete when we apply for a job are now stored in a computer in the many companies. The forms are a pain to fill out because they take so much time, but the data they contain can become very useful to us in the future by helping us to get a job. Many people who are employed by large companies can take advantage of these files simply by requesting that they be sent to a prospective new employer. This has given people in such companies an advantage over those who have had to develop and send out their own résumés when they decide to look for a new position.

With the advent of the personal computer, many more people can use its capabilities to construct their résumés and change them with a minimum of effort. Their personnel files can be as professional-looking and complete as those of anyone whose files are stored in computers in any large corporation. This gives many more people an advantage when they are looking for a job. In this way the computer has leveled out what used to be unequal advantages.

Let me share a personal example. Nearly a decade ago the church organization with which I worked installed a computerized personnel placement procedure. Every employee completed a form which contained work history, education, and skill data. This information was stored in the organization's computer and used when job openings became available in the organization or when employees wanted to submit a résumé to another organization. It was a good way for us and the organization to have composite records. (Unfortunately, when I left the organization, my résumé became my own responsibility. Until the personal computer became a reality, updating that résumé was a major and unwelcome task!)

The computer is beginning to work for new job hunters as well. An article in the May, 1983 issue of *Office Administration and Automation* described the way students at the Massachusetts Institute of Technology (M.I.T.) began to use a computer to match them with jobs this year. M.I.T. was the first university in the country to try such a procedure. Those who have used university placement bureaus know this has to be a much faster process than looking through job descriptions and going to many wasted hours of interviews.

One more use for computers in job searches is found in major urban newspapers, especially in the Executive Placement ads. Personnel placement companies talk about "matching your experience with the appropriate corporation". How do they meet this goal? They use computers to store and search information about personnel needs at major corporations. The search is conducted by computers programmed to look for certain characteristics and experiences potential employers require. If you sign up and match these characteristics and experiences, you could get the advertised job. If you don't qualify for any of the jobs in their computer searches, they will give you job and career counseling for a fee.

While many of us may not take advantage of our personnel files by looking for other jobs, the availability of computer searches is comforting. We know that, if we ever need a search, the computer can help us do it more efficiently and effectively.

Where Else Are You Stored?

There are many other places where your personal data may be stored. You may never know or even care where all these niches are. For example, those who taught in the state universities of Connecticut (and I suppose elsewhere) in the late 1960s and early 1970s had to be fingerprinted. When we put our prints on the blotters, new personal data files were opened on us and became a part of police and FBI records.

People who work in defense-related jobs are the subject of clearance checks, generally initiated by the FBI. Personal background data are verified, and some interviews are conducted for character references. These bits of information become parts of your personnel and police records.

A 1970 publication@ listed a dozen types of computer data banks that could contain information about each one of us. The twelve were police, regulatory, planning, welfare, financial, marketing, organizational, social, research, travel, service, and qualifications banks. These data banks serve medical, educational, marketing research, and charitable organizations. The data about us are used to target us for special promotions, insurance advertisements, financial opportunities, and special fund raising campaigns. Not much of what we are financially and credit-wise is not on some computer somewhere.

A more up-to-date discussion of where our data files might be found and used was in *USAIR* magazine for May, 1983. The article, "Putting Computers to Work," ± discussed the various uses certain kinds of industries make of the computer, and the problems and opportunities these uses have generated.

Social security data, a part of the government records for most of us. We are told to make changes every three years if we find mistakes because sometime every three or four years our data become composite and details before that are lost. The government gives us a chance to make corrections, but we are responsible for noting the errors.

Swapping Data

Access to our personal data is not limited to the financial community. The information we give on applications for loans and bank accounts is important to many companies that want to sell us something. The companies that have our data—for example, the personal information we file with a Visa Card application—regularly sell address lists to merchandising firms. They do not sell our personal data as such, but they include information about us in mailing lists that are attractive to other companies.

That's the reason we all periodically receive a form letter from credit card companies that tells us that the address lists of their customers are sold to other companies for promotion and sales purposes. If a person doesn't want the credit card company to sell our names to another company, all it takes is a signature and a check mark on the form letter. The point, however, is that our data, especially when aggregated with others, is a salable and marketable commodity.

Suppose, for example, that a publishing company is thinking

about creating a magazine for executives whose income is more than $40,000 a year. The publishing company could, of course, find composite information in the census materials on how many such executives exist. This isn't very helpful, however, because it is general and based on large amounts of data that have been compiled into averages. In addition, no names and addresses are given, which means the company has to go through another process to personalize the mailings. A better place to look for potential subscribers is in econometric data certain research firms collect. These data are costly, however, and they do not provide names and addresses either.

A third and much more accurate set of data can be found in the computer files of credit card customers. Since credit card customers are identified by name and address as well as according to financial information, our hypothetical publishing company can purchase a list of names and addresses and use direct mail marketing.

We might call the promotion and advertising we receive as second and third class mail "junk mail," but it is not that at all. It is carefully designed to get a response. A computer chose our name because our characteristics, income, expenditures, and possessions matched those of the target population. Our data were swapped for cash because we fit a desirable group. In the same manner, we can be excluded from lists because we do not have the characteristics an advertiser seeks.

This swapping can proceed only with our approval, but we don't know precisely what is being swapped. Suppose I asked a credit card company for my record. The company is obligated to provide the basic record, but it is not required to give me the categorizations under which I am listed on marketing lists. What I will get is what I already know. What the company keeps is what it has done with my data. In other words, my data may be personal but it becomes class oriented through computer manipulation. Once it is manipulated (nothing sinister), the data are no longer my personal property. The manipulated data are sold. I fit into a category, but I don't really know what that category might be.

The Privacy of Information Act forces companies to provide

me most of the data they have in my personal records, however. But it does not force them to let me see the categorized and salable information that is based on many records of which mine is one. I have access to a limited quantity of data, in other words.

The same thing happens with government information. If I question the government about its files, I can run into a limitation called classified data. This means that certain information cannot be released to anyone. Such data include security clearance interviews and the sensitive evaluations of some people.

The benefits of having data in the computer include ease of doing business, personnel job matching, and easy transfers of education and job histories to those who need that information. An important difficulty, though, in having data stored on us is that it can be used in such a way that we don't have access to it. We can find out the basics in the file but these rudiments in no way tell us who our data are being made available to. The issue of who controls aggregated personal data from which my name is selected and used is critical.

The form letter companies use to get permission to use my name and address is not adequate. With computers sitting on managers' desks and in homes where business offices might be located, personal data need to be more carefully protected. No longer are we discussing privacy of information the government or large corporations may have authority over. We are addressing moral issues: who has the right to purchase and use our stored data?

Getting Bad Data Out

We need to add that having personal data in a computer works to our advantage most of the time. We can do many things quickly because of these computers. On the other hand, many of us have had problems because those data banks contain bad information. When this happens, we can become very angry with those who straighten out our records.

The following conversation may remind you of some difficulties you have had with computers that contained inaccurate personal information:

"This letter is from the store where we applied for a credit card, dear. It says our application is denied because of the credit information supplied by the county credit bureau. I can't believe it! We don't have a bad credit history."

"Does it have an address or phone number for the credit bureau, John? Give them a call. We have to find out what they're spreading around about our credit."

"Yes. Here it is. I don't know where they get their information, but it has to be wrong."

A phone call righted the situation. The credit bureau had mixed this couple's good credit history with the poor record of an individual with the same name. After a few questions it became clear that the other person had a different address as well as a dissimilar credit history. The credit bureau's mix-up had led the store to reject the couple's credit card application. Happily, in this case the credit bureau sent revised information to the store with an explanation of the problem, and the couple was issued a credit card.

Another illustration concerns someone in California who was stopped for a minor traffic offense. Treated as a fugitive, he was handcuffed and put in jail. He was released in a short time, however; it seems that his name and general description matched those of a dangerous, wanted criminal. In spite of his efforts to clear his record, however, the police computer has still not been changed, and he still receives this treatment if he happens to be stopped for any reason.

Almost everyone who has used credit or been stopped for disobeying traffic laws could tell a similar story. When a computer operator makes a mistake, you pay a price. The displeasure we feel is understandable, yet a complex computer society is made even more complex by such computer errors. At such times we feel that it might be better to live in a less mechanized environment. That's a dream. We are in a computer-dependent society, whether we like it or not, and we must rely on the people who enter data into the computers and those who check on the accuracy of the records. When we are confronted with computer errors, most of the time computer operators, not computers, are at fault. The only thing the computer does is bring forth the information. It doesn't edit or enter it; people do.

Though this may be true, it doesn't relieve the frustration of trying to make changes in computer data. Have you ever tried to have inaccurate data or an incorrect charge deleted from your credit card record? It's not impossible, but the process certainly teaches one patience! Instructions on the bill tell you to write within a certain time and to a specific address. If you must call, a phone number is listed. If you call, you must answer questions to pass the security check. Then you will talk to someone who may or may not be able to assist you. You may be switched to two or three other persons. Finally you will be instructed in what to do to make the change.

Sometimes the instructions don't bring the results you hope for. The process must then be repeated, this time by letter. Eventually you may decide that those who work with the computer are as dumb as it is!

It may take several tries, but bad data can be removed from your personal files. Remember that in a computer society, making corrections in personal data files takes a lot of effort. The process may be complicated and time-consuming, but it eventually works.

However, there is another kind of problem that has emerged with the advent of personal computers in homes and offices. We can't make changes in data stored in those machines because we may not know they're there. Suppose you have succeeded in changing an error in a company's data bank. Let's say the error had to do with your personnel record. Is that record really changed? What if your manager has put your old personnel file on the small computer he keeps on his desk? He may not know about the change and continue to function with old data. Must he make the change? Who is to say? The existing laws have to do with the company records, not those kept by a manager on a small computer. Yet it is the manager who is making decisions about your raises and promotions based on data in his machine. How do you get the old data out of there?

This is a new area of concern. While laws govern what the

mainframes may keep protected and what each person has a right to see, they do not deal with data on us kept on small business and personal computers. These data may include such things as friendship groups, attitudes toward particular projects and people, and habits. Since the persons keeping the data are individuals, the laws do not touch what they are doing. Of course, if slander occurs, individuals have recourse. But subtle blackmail or pressure is not easy to prove in the courts.

Laws As Minimums

Ethics deal with standards of conduct. Laws, on the other hand, tend to express a basic or minimum level of conduct that, when broken, will result in some type of penalty. Disobeying an ethical code becomes important only when many people accept that code as a standard. For example, in the early West an ethical standard was to treat women with much respect and deference. On the other hand, the law treated women and men as equals. It was the ethical conduct code accepted by a majority of the settlers that permitted women privileges not accorded to men.

Our data are stored in many places. The small computer in the hands of unscrupulous managers or individuals can be used in all sorts of ways. For example, a computer terminal can be used to identify those who have recently purchased a luxury auto. If the terminal is in the hands of a criminal, the names and addresses of the owners and the kinds of accessories and dates of purchase are available. This makes stealing the autos only a matter of coordinating the thief's time schedule with when we're going to leave the auto unattended.

A neighbor with a personal computer can keep track of our comings and goings, our friends, and our evident purchases. These data might come in handy in legal situations or could be salable to certain kinds of people. We could find our homes robbed merely because the neighbor had kept track of us.

Laws dealing with privacy do not extend to individual computer operators. In fact, it might be possible to thwart an investigation of what we keep on our personal computers either at home or in the office by pleading that our privacy is being threatened. The law is a minimum in that it deals only with one small aspect of computer privacy. The larger societal good has not been addressed. Neither is there a strong enough ethic to allow more comprehensive laws to be enacted.

Another illustration relates to the copyright law. Assume a corporation purchases an expensive program for managers to project budgets, income, and expenditures. Many managers feel it is justifiable to have a personal copy of this program. They copy the program and distribute it to others because the company paid a premium for the original. They feel they have done nothing wrong. In fact, however, making duplicates of a copyrighted program diskette is pirating and is illegal. On the other hand, the most severe penalty a manager might expect is lack of back-up assistance from the software manufacturer when there is a problem with the program. This is hardly a deterrent.

Our computer-dependent society relies on people's honesty more than did the earlier industrial society. The machines of industry worked for us. Computers can work for us as well, but they are more people-dependent than are automated steel rolling mills. A computer, especially one controlled by managers and individuals, needs a person to direct it. The computer is not a substitute person. Therefore, the law and morality in a computer society must become more people-directed. People will be the guilty parties in whatever illegal or immoral acts the computer is given to do.

Chapter 3

DECISION-MAKING

As a graduate student my major project was to develop a way to predict the magnitude and kind of changes that might occur in social institutions, particularly the church, in a rural area in which a steel mill was to be built. I collected data, made projections, and developed indices of acceptance of social change. I then tested the projections and indices, using historical data. The planning groups in the area did their work as well. Everyone was prepared for significant change because of this new plant's location.

We could have saved ourselves a lot of time and effort, however. The steel mill, a new kind of rolling mill, was completely automated and the amount of social change it generated was negligible. The increase in population in the county due to the mill totalled fewer than 200 people. It was hardly noticed, even in this rural area. The commands that operated the mill—such things as steel sheet thickness, heat, cooling, and run times—were controlled by computers several hundred miles away. Supervisors in this mill were regulators of automatic controls while the other employees did maintenance and general labor work. Measurable social impact was due not to the number of people working at the new mill but to the increase in heavy truck traffic.

The fact that the activities of a steel mill would be controlled many miles away made a profound impression on me and the residents of the rural area in which the cold steel rolling facility was located. What the people resented most about the publicity hype preceding the mill's construction, the costs for securing the land, and the governmental clearances needed for the disposal of wastes that they helped the company with was the fact that the employees working in the mill were required to make minimal decisions. They could almost have been robots. A strike couldn't close the plant because so few people were needed to operate it. Besides, the operators would be supervisors, not union members. Being a pawn in the hands of an impersonal and unseen company grated on these independent rural residents.

That was back in the 1960s. We have moved light years into the future since then, because computers can now control many things remotely, including satellites years after they are launched from the earth. Such a feat is commonplace today, but most of us in the 1960s did not even consider it possible. The issue of control, important to those rural people then, has not gone away, however. They wondered, and we still wonder, who really has control of the decisions that most affect our lives?

Research firms make it their business to monitor our tastes and determine what makes us act the way we do. This information is sold to companies that then design products to sell us whether we want to buy them or not. While we have the option of whether or not to buy, we must realize that our economy is based on corporations that decide that we need to buy their products. Losing weight, growing hair on bald heads, using particular types of exercise equipment, wearing certain kinds of clothing, owning and driving automobiles that reflect a particular lifestyle, or eating breakfast foods that give us a jump on the day are all examples of how products that someone thinks we can be made to purchase encroach upon our lives. The producer has decided what is good for us, and many of us respond by buying his products.

Positioning, being in the market place first with the best, is the name of the game for corporate marketing managers. It is such a marketing process that controls many of our decisions. These decisions by corporate managers would not be possible without the data kept on people's ideas and opinions in the computers of various research firms. The managers know about us and decide what we can be sold. They use computer data to control our appetites.

Another type of decision mechanism may be taking hold of our schools. Legislation that gives tax breaks to computer companies that donate computer systems to school districts has made it possible for many school children to become acquainted with and use personal computers. The problem is that those computer companies are dictating, through a clever marketing procedure, that schools need and must use computers. The computer companies that have machines to sell make the decisions. The schools know they need to be engaged with computers, but their desire to work at this change carefully and on their own time schedule is thwarted. The computer companies are deciding, and thus controlling, when schools need computers.

It isn't necessarily a bad thing that our schools are training teachers and students in computer skills. That's not the point. The issue is control. The control can be subtle, as in peer pressure on principals and teachers, but it is control, nevertheless. When one group takes decision-making from the hands of another, the issue of control is important. That's what is happening now in this arena.

Dealing with schools and teaching raises another interesting issue. Computers can do and educate only as they are programmed to do and educate. The discussion of "Super Computers" in the July 4, 1983, issue of *Newsweek* pointed out the difficulties of a machine making human decisions. Yet, people think a computer can do their deciding for them. Typing programs that measure stroke time, errors, and speed are good, but they cannot decide whether a person is interested in or has an aptitude for typing. Humans make those decisions, based on personal interaction. A machine may be programmed to make certain kinds of decisions, but they are not human decisions.

A problem we humans face is our lack of awareness of the power of the computer to make decisions for us. Even as we subscribe more willingly to its use as an educational tool, those who do the programming may be lessening our ability to make crucial decisions. It isn't that we won't have more data on which to make an informed judgment. Indeed, we must admit that we have more information that we can use in many cases. The issue is much more subtle than that. It is retaining our control over decisions that affect us and our well-being as people.

Our human prerogative, as compared to that of a machine, is the development of decision-making capacities. Machines, computers included, have been invented to *help people,* not deprive them of their human capabilities. Unfortunately, we can become so enthralled with the computer that we fail to understand it as a machine. Thus, when we allow a programmer to develop computer instructions that relieve us of decision-making powers, we disallow the use of human emotion in critical areas of human conduct. For example, an article in *USA Today* (July 27, 1983, page 3A) quotes the dean of admissions of a California university as saying that computers ought to pick students for admission to college. He was refuted by a Michigan admissions officer who was quoted as saying, "Computers aren't very smart. I can synthesize very subtle information that a computer can't." The battle these two persons are fighting has to do with a more efficient way of admitting students. Should admission be based only on scores and tests of various sorts, or should humans be allowed to make judgments that use information other than test scores as part of the admittance criteria.

Computers are machines that do what people tell them to do. They can help us decide between alternative courses of action so long as we establish the criteria for those choices. The computer should not lull us into thinking that we don't need to cultivate among computer users, makers, and teachers an awareness of the limits of the machine to understand human emotions and personal needs. As we discuss decision-making from the standpoint of ethics, we must be sensitive to both the positive and negative potential which this tool holds for those of us doing planning, modeling, and deciding about finances, families, cities, groups, and people. The machine should not be allowed to rule us or disregard our needs as humans.

Enhanced Decision-Making Capacilities

An executive in a large corporation said, "The biggest change I've noticed in managerial decision-making in the past few years has come because of the personal computer. Now managers can look at spread sheets and make projections immediately without having to wait a week or two while the data-processing department spins the information out of the mainframes. We can do it now. That makes our people more informed managers and we get decisions in hours rather than having to wait a week or two."

This was the theme of an article, "The Micro-Mainframe War", in the June, 1983, issue of *Popular Computing*. The gist of the article was that data-processing departments are concerned that home computer operators and managers will be as able as they to access and manipulate data. The data-processing department managers feel threatened because those who need the data can get it quickly and make decisions days and weeks before the mainframes can spew out the information.

Immediate access to information should certainly enhance decision-making, especially within corporations. For example, corporate financial files are available to certain managers to access by personal computers at night. The theory is that they can develop strategies and formulate plans using these data without the added stress of waiting until the morning when other pressures are grasping for their attention. The companies that allow this kind of data use may be aware of the issue of security, but the misuse of information is presumed not to be a problem.

As consumers, we have begun to notice these increased capabilities when we have called a company with a problem about a bill or a question about our order. The individual on the other end of the phone can call up our records from the computer and make corrections while we are still on the line. It doesn't take weeks or months. For example, an individual had been receiving a utility bill that contained only his first name. This had gone on for several years in spite of periodic letters that he sent to the utility company. During the past year there was an overcharging problem with the bill, so he called about it. The person who answered the phone not only made the correction on the bill but also changed his name to the correct one! Having immediate access to data allowed the manager of customer relations to please this consumer.

Consider another possibility of enhanced decision-making, this time in the medical field. A doctor is confronted with symptoms that do not quite fit any disease she has confronted before. She uses the computer terminal in her office to connect to the medical diagnostic center and enters the symptoms. Within two minutes she receives on the screen in front of her the probable disease, references to documents that describe it, and possible methods of treatment. This kind of data retrieval may mean life or death to the patient. Without immediate access through the computer, such information would not be of benefit to this patient.

The "Super Computers" article described two software packages that allow field operators with a malfunction in a machine to call up instructions and pictures to solve most of their problems. The software package allows a company to capture and use the intelligence of one expert through a computer package. This obviously increases the efficiency of the company and will translate into improved earnings. It is likely that such software packages will become more commonplace as experience with them improves their capabilities.

Improved decision-making capabilities are a possibility with the aid of stored data and the speed with which computers can find such information. Making decisions from the data, however, is a human art and should not be entrusted to a machine. Neither should individuals be conned into thinking that corporations or a government can make better decisions. Securing information and weighing alternatives can be part of the drudgery machines can handle.

Machines, especially computers, can be programmed to mimic human capacities. However, the ethical issue is one of control. Who makes the decision? When that question is answered, the issue of control is isolated.

Concentrating on Making Decisions

"There are two types of researchers. The first is the person who has to make calculation after calculation. He is afraid to make decisions, so he gets immersed in the trivia of the data. The second is the person who wants to make decisions and depends on the computer to sort and compute. What I want you to be is the second type. Why waste energy on tedious details when a machine does it so much faster and never gets tired? Be smart! Focus your attention on decisions!"

This advice from a professor to graduate students was the motto under which use of the computer became second nature to those of us who worked with him at Northwestern University. It was the late 1960s, and the group was mixed. Some were students who had continued in school without working outside the student environment. Others of us had worked in business or other occupations and were returning for a higher degree.

Our experience didn't make any difference to him and did not affect his advice. That advice was practical. He wanted us to use our intelligence rather than become simply proficient users of calculators. In his mind, the function of a computer was to assist us to sort and manage information. Once we had the information in a particular form, it could help us make decisions. Making decisions was something we could do. Decision-making was not, for him, the function of a computer.

He would have had something to say in that difference of opinion we mentioned earlier between the two admissions officers. He would have told them they didn't know how to use the computer if they were asking it to make decisions. This might not have pleased the one admissions counselor who wanted to allow the computer to decide who was to be admitted to the university. On the other hand, he would have applauded the other officer who felt the proper function of the computer was to sort and store data. He could ask the computer for information that would shape his decisions. This latter individual used the computer to relieve him of much of the drudgery of the storage and retrieval of data, and let him concentrate on what he felt he could do well — make decisions about who was going to be admitted and who was going to be rejected.

Nevertheless, the argument that a computer would be less biased and more able to deal with large amounts of information is important to consider. The construction of super computers will assist in speeding up the process of making the calculations necessary for such complex tasks as weather forecasting and computer circuitry design. Only a machine can be programmed to perform the many computations quickly. Yet, the function of a human mind is decision-oriented, whereas the computer's capacity to remember and rapidly manipulate data makes its primary function storage and retrieval. A computer can enhance decision-making by allowing people to concentrate on making decisions.

For example, a pilot can be trained through the use of computer controlled simulators. The various possibilities of wind, mechanical failures, midair collisions, and sabotage are programmed into the simulator. The potential pilot is forced to make decisions when faced with disaster in the air, on the ground, or as the plane is landing. The controlled cockpit becomes a crucible in which he or she must concentrate on decision-making. This use of computers does not take decisions away from humans. It rather assists them in developing their potential for quick decisions. Not only that, computers allow the trainees to see the results of their decisions.

This same kind of instant retrieval of data allows a child to know when he or she gives the correct answer to a math problem or a language student to know when the translation of a word is incorrect. The same principles of storage and manipulation of data allow a builder to calculate the amount of supplies it will take to complete a structure, or the instructor of a spelling class to know which students need more assistance.

In each of these illustrations, an individual must be able to read the data from the computer and make decisions that have consequences that affect other people, be they students, purchasers, or parents. Instructors, builders, and learners can have access to the data, but they must make the decisions.

Machines Making Decisions

Even if we recognize that people are primary decision-makers, it is important to realize that computers are involved in decision-making as well. For example, a feature of some automobiles is a computer that calculates the correct mixture of fuel and air, based on driving conditions at any given time. The advertisement even suggests that the computer saves you fuel! The computer not only computes data, but it makes instantaneous decisions that adjust the fuel intake, so the claim is not so farfetched as it may sound.

Some computer owners depend on their computer to take care of their home and lawn. Their computers are programmed to turn the lights on and off, activate and shut off the automatic sprinkler system in the lawn, and be the alarm system for a home. The computer makes the decisions on each of these items based on the time at which its internal clock was set.

What really happens in these and similar situations is that humans have programmed into computers a decision-making process. It is a process that reads, "If this condition occurs, do this." The process is relatively straightforward and is based on cause and effect. The decisions are simple, even though their programming may take hours to perfect and be quite complex. People set the instructions; the computer slavishly follows those instructions. Even when confronted with these facts, people are prone to think that computers can make intelligent decisions.

Come into a studio in which city planning is taking place. A computer is working hard to produce alternative scenarios of city neighborhoods based on the kinds of industrial, commercial, and housing types the planners feed into it. The designs will include streets, utilities, and needed services. The computer can assist the planner in decision-making by showing alternatives that can be developed on the basis of the data. The computers are often so intriguing that planners allow them to make decisions, rather than base a design on human feelings and preferences. That's the reason so many plans, encased in elaborate booklets, have graced bookshelves and not been implemented.

Designers of automobiles and airplanes face practical economic constraints. Their products must be within a feasibility budget, or else the design is not useful. This doesn't stop the designers from tinkering and dreaming. Unfortunately for some designers at some auto companies, they did not listen carefully to the consumer in the late 1970s. These companies lost business because of the styling, lack of safety, and fuel consumption of their autos. Other companies listened to the people and did not allow computers to make their decisions for them.

Those who work with modeling on computers can be lured into thinking the computer has more capabilities than it possesses. It is fascinating to look at models of any type and be captivated by what the computer has produced. A strong inclination is to believe what it shows to be the truth, when in fact it is merely a compilation of data. The computer of today has some of the same fascination as the nymphs who lured sailors to their death on the rocks in the Greek fables. The computer can seduce us into thinking we are more powerful and talented than we are. Just because it produces what we want it to put forth, it does not make the product correct or right. A machine is a machine in spite of what it can do with graphics and design. Unfortunately, we humans often forget this fact of life.

The ethical problem in all this is that those who sell and make use of computers emphasize what it can do and forget to tell people its limitations. Neither do they suggest that the human mind has capabilities more unique than anything yet put into a computer. It may be that someday computers will be a match for the human brain, but that can come only when it can synthesize data as quickly as the brain, which receives many different kinds of stimuli at the same time. Until humans program the computer to match human capabilities, it is still a machine. This fact must be stressed to those of us who purchase and use them. We must not forget our capabilities just because the computer does many things faster than we can.

Losing Skills

George Orwell's novel *1984* painted a frightening picture of a life controlled by machines. The computer was hardly invented when the book was written, but one can now look at the scenario he wrote and see how quickly it could become a reality. Of particular importance is the ease with which people can become machine-dependent. It doesn't take much imagination to visualize a generation of young people who become so dependent on the computer that they lose their skills in mathematics. They could have difficulty in simple things such as adding, subtracting, multiplying, and dividing. Their attitude could be, "Why bother with those things when the computer can solve every problem we face?"

Think about the skills we could lose because we depend too much on the computer. It has a dictionary to check my spelling, so why should I worry about spelling? There is a program that searches libraries for books and articles that I need when I'm writing, so why should I learn how to use a library? There are programs that plan meals for me so why should I learn about nutrition? The list could be extended into business, education, and other aspects of life. Why should we learn these skills if a computer can do the job for us?

Consider a ballplayer. He or she can be aided by the data on hitting and fielding that a computer maintains on him or her, but there is no way the computer can stand at the plate and hit the ball. In the same vein, why should it be necessary to allow ourselves to be illiterate just because a computer has the capacity to do many of the things we feel are unnecessary? The human mind is too precious to let stagnate on account of a computer. We can lose skills, but the ethical question is, do we have a right to be that lazy?

Another kind of skill relates to the arts. Music and art as well as dance are being programmed into computers. The computer allows an individual with limited talent to learn and create. This is a step in the right direction. On the other hand, there is something unique in the smell and activity of an art studio that can't be duplicated by an artistic computer print-out. The skill of mixing paint to capture the hue of a sunbeam as an artist sees it should not be given to a computer. Yet, these skills can be lost when they are no longer considered important or necessary.

One of the most difficult-to-understand courses I encountered in college was "Logic." It seemed illogical to me most of the time! Yet, it helped develop a thought process that has been a mainstay throughout my adult life. That kind of course could be dropped from the curriculum because there may be no need to have those skills in the age of the computer. When we need something organized, we can call on a computer database program and presto, the problem is organized for us. Those skills we worked so hard to gain may not be available to another generation.

The intent of this section is not to frighten but to alert us to some consequences of overdependence on computers. They can take over for us in many ways, but every time we become dependent on them, they control what we can do. Humans are so much more lively as companions and unpredictable as colleagues than any dumb machines. Why let them take away those skills we need to use every day? It doesn't make sense.

Computers as Work Companions

A corporation's typing pool is now giving way to a computer bin. This is a small cubicle in which is found a desk on which sit a computer and a display screen. Included are places to store materials, a holder for data that are to be entered, and a few other odds and ends. The operator of the computer enters this cubicle and works. He or she is discouraged from looking around because the sides of the cubicle are tall enough to conceal the other workers. Consequently, there is no talking. If one could look down on such a room, it would look like a large maze in which people are trapped.

The computer bin has special problems that corporations and unions are addressing. For example, some states are considering the regulation of the use of video display terminals, the screens on which words or whatever else an individual types into a computer are displayed. Such regulation is opposed, as one might expect, by the Computer and Business Equipment Manufacturers Association. The most important problems people experience are eyestrain and muscle strain, according to a survey noted in *Office Administration and Automation* (May, 1983, p. 24). The inflexible nature of computer terminals causes these difficulties. The terminals are not movable. Therefore, a person must concentrate on the screen while entering or reading data. In addition, the color of the screen and the figures on it can cause fatigue much more quickly than the black on white of type on a piece of paper. There is also some feeling that the computer worker needs more frequent breaks and time away from the machine than does the typist.

These physical constraints are being addressed. Yet an important factor, the lack of social interaction the bins create, has not been discussed. A normal typing pool allows people to have some personal communication with others. At the very least they had visual contact and a feeling that they were part of a group. The computer worker, sitting in a cubicle with no visual or verbal contact with other workers, is in danger of becoming an isolate whose communication with other workers can occur solely at check-in, check-out, and lunch time. Such infrequent opportunities for operators to have companionship may be a reason some companies are finding that these operators make more frequent visits to the nurse than do other types of employees.

The bins are a product of a computer mentality. Efficiency and increased productivity are more important than the needs of employees. Extend those corporate desires to employees who work on computers at home. There we discover that not only is the computer a work companion but it can also become a taskmaster. Homebound individuals must work more quickly and with fewer mistakes on a piecework salary than do those who are employed full time at the corporation's offices. In addition, homebound workers receive none of the benefits full-time employees receive. In some instances, these people, who receive none of the benefits and whose productivity is based on piecework, must rent the computers from the company in order to work at all.

Who benefits the most from such a setup? The corporation, on the whole. It saves on office space, salaries, and benefits. It also gets better productivity from the home workers. This does not discount the benefit to the employee who has to or prefers to work at home. The primary ethical concern has to do with equalizing the benefits the corporation and the employee receive. No one wishes to deny the corporation its profits. At the same time, a corporation that uses the talents and time of individuals, especially those who do the data entry work on which decisions must be made, ought to reward them with benefits and salaries worthy of their importance to the corporation. Without quality data entry, no one in the corporation, including planners, presidents, or members of the board, would be able to do a specific task well.

There is another side to the issue, however. Some individuals prefer to have a computer to another person as a work companion. They tend to become so intrigued with the machine and what it can help them accomplish that they find it more interesting than human beings. It becomes important at this point to find ways to help computer-bound workers break the chain that links them to a machine. Addiction, as mentioned earlier, is as much a problem with a computer as it is with alcohol or drugs. Society has not felt it worthwhile to discourage computer addiction; rather, most forces in society push people toward increased computer use.

Reliance on Standardized Tests and Diagnosis

Anyone who has looked at college entrance requirements recently knows that one or two sets of standard test scores are required for admission. The scores must fall within a predetermined range each college or university sets before a candidate will be considered. Computers may not make the tests or the decisions, but they and the tests are important factors. Decision-making is based on standardized test scores.

Test scores reflect, in spite of what some advocates might suggest, cultural background, language experience, and personal interest. The scores do have some predictive value in college because the curricula are established and taught in a standardized fashion. Individuals must conform or they will not remain students very long.

Psychological examinations based on standardized tests are a normal procedure for some professional schools. These exams, it is felt, will eliminate persons who have psychological problems that will make it impossible to function successfully in the profession. Many of us have friends who have passed those exams, only to spend inordinate amounts of money and time in counseling offices afterwards, however. The tests did not isolate evident problems, nor did they help the individuals move into careers in which they could succeed.

Diet and exercise regimes are based on standardized needs more often than on individual peculiarities. The "normal" weight according to height and body structure frustrates many people who have a "normal" weight at variance with that on the chart. They live full and active lives, in spite of being above or below the weight on the chart. The chart succeeds only in making them feel inadequate and abnormal.

We could use other kinds of illustrations of how standards and tests that have been compiled by computers govern our lives. We have allowed these standardized tests and charts to tell us what we ought to be and how we should be acting. While we have not developed a totally conforming society, it will not take much more reliance upon the computer to be close to the *1984* mold. Regardless of what we believe, so long as those standardized tests are used to make decisions about and for us, the computers are in control and we aren't. The mean score or weight is governing how we should think, act, and feel. That's scary!

A computerized society without ethics is like an automobile without a body. It runs, it goes fast, and it gets to a destination. Unfortunately, there is no protection for the person who is guiding or operating the car. The driver is totally wrapped up in getting the machine to go. When operating a machine becomes an obsession, individuals and society forget about the persons and groups that are supposed to benefit by it. We are at that point with the computer. It is time to think about people. It's time to set some ground rules for ethics in a computer-dependent society!

Chapter 4

GROUND RULES FOR ETHICS IN A COMPUTER SOCIETY

"Get three kids together, and the first thing they do is make rules. They have to know what the territory is and what they're expected to do," one of my neighbors remarked recently.

"I've noticed that, but the same thing happens in most meetings I attend. We aren't kids, but we need to understand our roles and limits just like the kids. I guess people need rules," I replied.

Developing ethics for a computer society is not like playing a game of tag at dusk. In tag, the number of players is limited, we can see them, and we usually know them. In a computer society the number of players is in the millions, we will see very few of them, and we don't know them. If it takes ground rules to have an orderly game of tag with a few friends, the magnitude of computer use in our society dictates even more the need to abide by some ethical guidelines. As in every game, ground rules describe the territory or conditions under which the game is to be played, identify who the players might be and their roles, suggest behavior principles for everyone, and indicate possible penalties.

Previous chapters have suggested the kinds of players involved and the territory that ethics needs to address. The fact that computers are in many homes and on the desks of many managers has removed the machine and its capabilities from the sole possession of computer professionals. Now nonprofessionals operate computers. There is nothing intrinsically wrong with this. In fact, the move from a small group benefitting and controlling the computer to many people using it to solve a multitude of problems is a good thing. The difficulty arises with how the users govern themselves. Professionals have an ethical code[1], but the rest of us aren't certain of the "rights" and "wrongs" of computer use. We don't yet have such a code to help us.

Previous discussions have shown that people can become addicted to the computer, with serious consequences to marriages and other human relationships. Being so involved in the programming and operation of a personal computer that one's social and emotional life is hindered is a serious side effect of owning or operating a personal computer. No warning has been given, nor has this potential problem been suggested, to the millions of new owners of personal computers. They need to be warned and given ways to cope with computer addiction.

Another part of a code of computer ethics is deciding who monitors what is put into personal computers, be they in the home or in an office. Users could view such monitoring as an invasion of privacy. Yet they may be entering, storing, and retrieving data that could be detrimental to friends, neighbors, and associates. How one determines what data are allowable and legitimate for personal computers is another important aspect ethical guidelines need to cover.

Theft is not a nice word when all we mean is pirating a computer program, but the word is accurate. When people take something that doesn't belong to them without giving credit or paying for it, that's stealing. It's stealing to copy a copyrighted computer program just as surely as it is shoplifting a pair of shoes. It's also stealing to break a security code to a bank, a school's grading system, or the phone company in order to withdraw money, change grades, or charge long distance calls. These are crimes people who have access to personal computers can easily commit. Many times these crimes are an individual's response to a dare or a challenge to see what computers can do. Such behavior indicates that the individual has no feeling for limits to what should and should not be the legitimate function of a computer. Ethics must deal with this issue.

Problems relating to dependence on the computer to the detriment of generating and honing personal skills are another part of the territory of computer ethics. Some people can become so dependent on the computer that they lose the ability or motivation to learn. This is especially dangerous when computer programs erode thinking and decision skills. After all, computer programs are the creation of other people. Who says that what they wrote as a way of organizing or deciding is appropriate for everyone else's situation?

Another part of the territory relates to those who sell computers. This includes manufacturers, sales personnel who deal only with corporations, and retail outlets. Not one of these groups has assumed that its responsibilities include more than making available a product and providing a limited warranty on it. The issues of inadequate training of sales personnel, lack of service for products sold, education of the consumer in how to use and how not to use the product, and what ought to be kept on the computer have not been of concern. Yet, these are issues that can be serious problems to a computer-dependent society. Ethics must deal with manufacturers and merchandisers.

Teaching computer literacy, a great bonanza for some consultant firms, is too serious to be left to entrepreneurs alone. A brochure came in the mail recently describing a week of training. One of the sessions was entitled "Attitude Engineering," which, the description said, "will examine the human issues critical for success." This discription does not suggest that the session would be overly concerned with ethical considerations.

The place to look for courses on ethics isn't consultant firms. Nor are school systems much better equipped to handle ethics. Yet schools are entrusted with millions of young people who must become computer literate during the next few years. Ethics has to become a part of all such training.

The groups that need to be concerned about ethics, then, include users, suppliers, and trainers involved with computers, especially personal computers. Some people will suggest that a start has been made on establishing guidelines by legal means. They will point to new legislation in the areas of copyrights and privacy of information. However, privacy and copyright, as these apply to corporations and government, are only a small segment of the problem. The much broader need is to make the millions of us who use and own personal computers ethically conscious as we become computer literate.

We need to know, the same as professional computer operators in large installations, that we are governed by laws and peer pressure. Laws are important because agencies can enforce them. Peer pressure helps to enforce ethical behavior. Therefore, a code of ethics for a computer-dependent society will be only as effective as we users allow it to become. Guidelines for creating an ethical code that can guide us in our computer-dependent society are needed.

Computers Are Tools

The *New York Times,* in its "Business Day" section of May 11, 1983, reported on several surveys of home computer users. Defining "home computers" as those that retail for less than $1,000, the surveys indicated that a majority of the users purchased their computers so they could play games. However, almost half reported that they used their computers primarily for business or office homework, or as a child's or an adult's learning tool. Those whose purchase totalled more than $1,000 were likely to have a machine that was not used primarily for games, but was either work or home oriented. These people understand the computer as a tool.

USA Today on August 3, 1983, reported on studies about "couples with high-tech tension." The article reported on how couples were coping with the computer addiction of one partner in a marriage. The article contained two small suggestion boxes of advice from psychologists on how to live with an individual who is compulsive about computers. People who are compulsive about computers tend not to understand that it is a tool.

Stevens Institute of Technology in Hoboken, New Jersey, required eighty freshmen to purchase microcomputers and bring them to school in the fall of 1982. *All* freshmen entering in 1983 will be required to purchase and bring computers with them, as will freshmen at Clarkson College.[2] They represent the vanguard of the future when many colleges will require all their students to own and use computers. These colleges know that computers are tools that can assist students to be more creative.

The computer is a tool in the same way that a tractor or an electric saw or a food processor is a tool. A tool assists an individual accomplish a task more quickly and efficiently than is possible without it.

Those who have a romantic idea of horse and buggy days have usually not had an opportunity to try to plough hard packed dirt with a team of horses or mules. When the tractor became commonplace, farming became a business, not a family industry. The difference in what could be accomplished using the same number of people was phenomenal. Additional improvements to the power of the tractor allow one person to plow, harrow, fertilize, and plant on each trip down a field. Each of these tasks used to be a separate operation when farmers had to depend on horses or mules.

Few of us associate a computer with a tractor, yet they are both tools. The difficulty we have in considering a computer a tool is that we can manipulate it so easily. It seems to respond readily to what we do to it, so some people regard it as an extension of themselves. It does, of course, have capabilities that make it user oriented. It can be controlled easily, and it does what it is asked to do. Nevertheless, it is not an extension of a personality. It is a machine, nothing more, and nothing less.

What difference does thinking of the computer as a tool make? It means we become emotionally detached from it and its power. Not many of us are emotionally attached to a typewriter to the extent that we want to sit in front of it for hours on end. Neither are we enthralled by calculators. But we can be absorbed in a problem, or in writing, or in reading. These activities are not machines, they are mind-stretching experiences. The difficulty we have in separating ourselves from a computer is that we can use it to become absorbed in mind-stretching experiences. Because of its capacities to store, recall, and manipulate data, it allows us to solve difficult problems, write and talk with others by electronic means, and develop routines for business and household tasks we never dreamed we could do.

Since the computer gives us more power and control, we tend to regard it as more than a machine. It is a mystical box that calls from us qualities we didn't think we had. That it can help us develop our potentials in thinking and problem-solving is undeniable. What is debatable is that we would not have developed those potentials without the computer, had we applied as much time and energy doing so before we purchased one. We must remember that the computer is a tool, not a magical box that unlocks talents. People must still work hard at learning and practicing skills. This work may be more pleasant and fulfilling when a computer is being used, but it is the work, not the machine, that is the key to accomplishment.

Another danger must be avoided, the danger of making a computer a substitute person. A computer is a "safe" companion in that it does what it is asked to do. It doesn't nag, whine, criticize, or belittle. It doesn't change moods or get tired. It can go as long as a person wants it to run. It doesn't talk back. These are characteristics human beings don't always exhibit. If an individual wants to live in a completely positive "social" environment, a computer can provide it. Unfortunately, such a person becomes less a person, because he or she can't grow as a result of human interaction. There isn't human interaction when a computer takes the place of people.

Those who have already made the computer their substitute personal companion must be diverted by others who know that the computer is a tool. Never, in a society that is computer-dependent, should an individual be allowed to let a machine become a substitute for human relationships.

The first ground rule, then, is to realize that computers are tools. They must be treated the way machines are treated. They are mystical in the same way that electricity, television, and automobiles are mystical. They help us when we use them correctly. They are dangerous when we grant them too much power and allow them to have dominion over us.

Understand the Computer

A "partnership of human beings and computers could promise infinite betterment for mankind if man's understanding of how to use the computer was a well-balanced one."[3] Ashley Montagu and

Samuel S. Snyder, who write the book this quotation appears in, discuss our need to understand the computer. They attempt to encourage people to learn about the capabilities of the computer and how to use it to solve human problems. Of particular importance to them was creating a more livable future.

"I'm going to take a course on computers at the community college this fall. I've got to learn about them to see if I can use one in my work," a friend of mine said to his neighbor recently.

"The best way to learn about them is to buy one and use it for a particular job. That way you'll get a feel for what it can and can't do," the neighbor replied.

"I don't function like that. I have to think about something, discuss it, and make my decision later. It's just the way I am."

Each of these persons wants to use a computer to help him do his work better. He may be rather skeptical about it as a personal tool, and regard it with a slight sense of awe. That's not unusual since his primary contact with computers has been through corporations that use computers to do his banking and billing transactions. Changing his perception of how he can use a computer can be a slow process.

Contrast their reluctance to the enthusiasm of a new owner of a personal computer. He is convinced that the computer will be his—if not the world's—salvation! He is likely to say something like this: "You can't believe what I can do now that I have this computer. I can get in touch with people anywhere in the country and carry on conversations. I can buy things cheaper than I could at any store. I can keep records, get into libraries, and a host of other things. I don't know how I lived without it!"

His enthusiasm will hopefully be tempered as he spends the hours necessary to learn how to use his computer. Even so, he could become even more convinced that it can save him from a banal existence. The more some people learn how to manipulate a computer, the more convinced they become that it is critical to their survival. That's not true, but advocates of computers are not easily shorn of their convictions.

Charles Rubin in the August, 1983, issue of *Personal Computing* tells us why some people are afraid of computers. His contention is that undue fear of them is unfounded and, when viewed as tools to assist in getting work done, they can be a significant addition to an individual's work scene. The person who operates a computer is in control of it, not the other way around. People ought to understand the computer as a tool that they can use.

Several magazines have begun publication since the advent of the personal computer. Many of them relate to a particular personal computer such as the Apple or IBM, though some are more general. Each magazine wants to inform and instruct the owner of a personal computer in its use and capabilities. Several of the magazines contain program listings that individuals may copy and run on their computers. A description of the specific tasks the programs can perform is included in articles that precede the listings. The magazines attempt to help people understand and operate the computer they have purchased.

An important part of each such publication is a discussion of new programs ("software") that have recently become available and new attachments ("hardware") that can be used with a particular brand of personal computer. Directions indicate how easy programs are to operate and how well the owner's manual describes them. The same kind of directions are given for new pieces of equipment. The magazines, in this fashion, attempt to fill in niches of knowledge for personal computer owners.

As important as these magazines are, however, they are pro-computer and assume its validity. These publications are not particularly concerned about ethics, although the tone of their editorials assumes an ethic that does not condone any illegal use of the machines. Their editors are interested in increasing the kinds of uses people make of personal computers. In the pages of the magazines are found an interesting variety of stories relating to how someone has been innovative with his personal computer. Competition between computer manufacturers and the agreement between their advertisements and the functions of their machines are discussed as well. Yet, very few articles that deal with ethics and computer use have appeared in these — or other — magazines. Somehow it seems that understanding the computer does not include, at least for these publications, informing people about ethical behavior in a computer-dependent society.

In spite of this deficiency, these magazines help people understand the computer. While some of the articles are glowing affirmations of computers, most of the writers are careful to present a balanced view of the capabilities and limitations of hardware and software. The magazines may be procomputer, but they strive to help people understand the computer.

This is in sharp contrast to some salespersons in computer stores. Their interest is purely in making a sale. They emphasize the capacity of the computer without touching on its limitations. When you listen to some salespersons you would think the machine could do everything, even without someone controlling it! The salesperson will often try to sell you a variety of programs for the machine without a clear idea of your own specific needs. Such salespersons—and there seem to be legions of them—are not helpful in assisting you to understand the computer.

"We can't use it properly if we don't know what it can do." These were the words of one man as he cut off a salesperson in midsentence. We must first learn what a computer can and can't do. This is prerequisite to operating it correctly and effectively for the tasks we have in mind. You have to know what the computer can do before you can develop an ethics for a computer society as well.

Therefore, the second ground rule for ethics in a computer-dependent society is to understand the capabilities of your computer. This may mean becoming computer literate, but it is a literacy that balances the positives and negatives. The computer is neither a threat nor a panacea for humankind. As a tool it can be manipulated to create both promises and dangers for people. The aim of understanding is to emphasize the promises and minimize the dangers. This is the kind of understanding of computers that an ethic is trying to cultivate.

Controlling Computers

The manager was fuming. "Every time I ask for a report, it's 'We can't do it til next week, Mr. Jones.' They have to make sure the program works. I don't get it! The program worked the last time I asked for the report, and that was only three weeks ago!"

Most people who have made requests of computer installations can understand Mr. Jones' frustration. There seems to be a continual delay in accomplishing even the smallest tasks. The delay may be due to an equipment malfunction, a lack of paper, the absence of an ill employee, or any of a host of other reasons. The excuses seem to mount in direct proportion to the urgency of the request!

Commenting on this phenomenon recently, an executive said, "Managers have got to realize that when they talk to computer installations, they're talking to technicians and not managers. Technicians think differently and act differently from managers. The technician's concern is to make a report look nice and be precise with the data. A manager's concern is to make decisions. The data have to be good, but the report need be little more than readable."

His point was that when a corporation entrusts its computer facility to technicians, it should expect a technician's response to a request. It will be forthcoming, but on the time schedule of the technician, not according to the requested deadline of the manager. So long as technicians control the system, managers will be at their mercy.

When managers get their own terminals and can tap into the mainframes, things change drastically. That was the issue discussed in "The Micro-Mainframe War".[4] Technicians became concerned that managers would no longer be dependent on their skills and talents. The main issue, however, had to do with control. Who has control of the data is at the heart of this war and may be the basic issue in several similar wars in the future.

The control of data is the issue around which the privacy of information legislation was crafted. Companies, it decided, could keep records on individuals so long as people could examine and correct those records. No longer could a company with impunity give out information without the knowledge or agreeement of an individual. While this issue has not been satisfactorialy reconciled for many, it at least began the discussion of who has a right to control computer records. That legislation, however, does not adequately acknowledge, much less address, the control of data in personal computers.

An interview with an automation expert in the August 1, 1983, issue of *U. S. News and World Report* contained this observation: "Expansion has come so fast that many companies have no idea how many terminals they have. And with more people having access, the chances for crime and security breaches increase."[5] Once control passes from the mainframes to the personal computers in corporations, many problems can follow. Dealing with those problems is a critical ethical concern.

Control raises another important issue related to people. The computer operator and programmer should be sensitive to people and not compress people into standardized molds. That is the message some personal computer makers and programmers have heard recently. They have begun to advertise machines and software that are "user friendly." This means some of the jargon has been eliminated and people can understand what the machine needs to make it work properly.

This may be of some consolation to the computer user. It doesn't, however, begin to deal with the rest of the population whose lives have been recorded on standardized forms for years. We are a standardized people because technicians decided that their format was the only way our characteristics and attitudes could be recorded, stored, and manipulated by computers. These technicians still control us, unfortunately. An ethic for a computer-dependent society must confront the issue.

The ethic must deal with how we can access not only the data in corporate and government computers, but also their aggregate use of our information. We need to know how we are categorized and the firms that are purchasing our names and addresses. This may take freedom of information too far, but anything less is allowing our data to be manipulated by technicians and sold by marketers. There may be no harm in such an arrangement, but it seems that if the corporation is to profit because of us, we ought to have some idea how our data are packaged to be so attractive.

Personnel files, educational backgrounds, and character interviews are protected from the possibility of our inspection. Technicians have created levels of security that must be passed before these pieces of information are available to anyone, including ourselves. A computer ethic must take the initiative and demand access to data about us from the technician. People need to deal with people, not be standardized or computerized without being able to find out what is in their files. Protestations aside, the threat to privacy is more real today than it was a few years ago. That threat is compounded by the fact that control of our files is in the hands of technicians who can release the information to managers but not to us.

Think for a minute about the danger of having your data in a personal computer on a manager's desk. That individual can add to or manipulate the data and send it to data banks without being caught by any security system. We could lose credit ratings, money, or records and not be aware of what has happened until some agency calls or we are booked for a crime. Or someone else could take our credentials and capitalize on them for their own benefit. Control of data and access to our files are part of the same issue; they must be part of a computer ethic.

The third guideline for a computer ethic must deal with who controls the computer. The ethic must emphasize that people who are sensitive to people ought to control computers and data, rather than placing total responsibility for large computer installations in the hands of technicians. By the same token, those whose primary concern is for people must instruct users of personal computers, not those who blindly fulfill the machine's needs for standardized data and instructions. This will require manufacturers and programmers to continue to develop more user-oriented and people-sensitive machines. In addition, the ethic must address the standardization of society so that we can begin to design new molds computer technicians have not created or determined. The emphasis on individualization and personal worth should be reflected in all parts of society, including computer use and dependency.

Protecting People Needs

"One of the most beautiful sights in the world is the sun comin' up over the mountains. You look out the window and bend your eyes over those hills, and a peace like a person never knows is possible takes over your body. I tell you, there's no place better to live." These words were spoken by a transplanted Appalachian native. He lives in a city now because there is no work for him back home. However, sometime during the year he will become discouraged, leave his job for a few days, and return home to those hills for personal refreshment. He has people needs that are greater than his need for a job or money.

"We both work, have our own careers, and find it difficult to schedule things so we have time together. About every four or five weeks we take a weekend together and devote it to us. Sometimes we go somewhere, and sometimes we stay home. The important thing is to be together and get back in touch." So said one couple who find stimulation and challenge in their separate careers, but recognize a commitment to each other that also needs to be nurtured. They feel and respond to people needs — their own.

"That was fun. We haven't been out for several months. It was good to get together with that group. We have a lot in common," the handsome, middle-aged New Englander said.

"You're right. We ought to be more social. It does something for us," his slim, attractive wife replied.

They were discussing a social evening with a group. They enjoyed it because it satisfied a need for people, social relaxation, and interaction.

A society that is computer-dependent must assure itself that these kinds of needs can and will still be met. High tech speed and hype creates transitory relationships. People meet, briefly interact, and move on. While we have enjoyed mobility in society for years, the feeling computers force on us is one of transitoriness. For example, an individual used to a computer's speedy calculations and instant response finds it difficult to listen to a slow-speaking associate make a point about sales. It is much easier to ignore the associate and have the computer make the point.

"Temporary" and "artificial" may describe the kind of social interaction a computer society creates. Permanence refers to anything that is two years old or more. Attitudes are governed by the current best seller's advice. A society based on speed cannot take the time to develop interpersonal relations. People interact with their computers. Relaxation is playing computer games. Such a society can easily conclude that social groupings are not important to people's health.

But people need to interact with each other. They need the stimulation that comes from sharing insights and ideas. And they need relaxation. With so many people working, it becomes even more important for such experiences to occur in the workplace as well as away from it. A corporation or organization that has to produce a product often feels that those who come to work should be expected only to produce that product. That's a short-sighted view of human effort. Motivation comes as people believe others care about them. They need input into the way their job fits into the whole. Take away these two feelings, and a company or organization will be faced with morale problems.

The computer is a slavish taskmaster. It records what we do as well as how quickly and accurately we do it. It can rank us against everyone else in the office or organization. By the computer's standards we may be a liability to a particular corporation or organization. We become expendable, in other words, because of those standards, even though our strong point is helping others become acclimated to their job and the company and being able to solve most of the conflicts that occur around us. These are attributes the computer's analysis of our skills may not reflect, but they are very important to have in any workforce.

The push is on in our state for upgrading the opportunities of "gifted" and "talented" students. Of course many parents believe these words describe all their children. How do you determine who is gifted and talented? In our school system today the decision is made by computer. Each child has several opportunities each year to participate in extra activities such as art, drama and writing workshops, and problem-solving discussion times. When a child attends one of these activities, his attendance is duly noted and becomes a part of his computerized school record. Administrators can then easily identify those who are gifted and talented. Such children take advantage of most of the extra activities.

The difficulty with such a system is that the activities may be dull, or scheduled on Saturdays, which are family days for many people. They may not relate to the interest levels of those who participate. That doesn't matter to some people. It is the students, not the administrators who created the activities, who are rewarded or penalized for their participation or failure to participate. It doesn't take overly perceptive parents to realize that attendance at these events is mandatory if their children are to be considered gifted.

The tendency to depend on such computer records and be guided by impersonal standards programmed into the computer are prevalent in our society. An ethic must confront this tendency and insist on putting people first. People need to be protected and listened to as they talk with one another, share ideas, and shape their personal futures. A computer-dependent society is too prone to ignore them and their needs. It may be more interested in compartmentalizing and standardizing.

In summary, the fourth guideline for ethics must be to recognize and protect people needs. The three most important needs, from the perspective of the development of a strong social group or society, are interaction, stimulation, and relaxation. An ethic is created for people. It must be people oriented. A computer society can destroy people because of its push for speed, impersonalism, and standardization.

The Family

The family is a very important concern in every society. It is the one social institution society depends upon to provide people respite from the pressures of life. It doesn't always function that way, of course. Some families can't help their members cope effectively with the external pressures of the society because they apply more pressure on the family members than society does. Nevertheless, the family is the group to which most of us turn for non-threatening interaction, relaxation, and stimulation. In the family most people find opportunities for personal recreation.

No institution in a complex society is immune to or protected from external pressures. And pressures take their toll. Each pressure on family life makes it more difficult for the family to help its members relieve, minimize, or counteract societal pressures. During the past three decades, for example, three electronic inventions have contributed greatly to the pressures on the family—television, video games, and personal computers. Separately, they have destroyed some families because one or more of their members have become addicted to them. They have become problems society has had to tackle.

Many experts and parents during the past two decades have felt that television has been a menace to family life. Their reasons for concern were admittedly legitimate. For instance, in some families, television was an electronic baby sitter for some young people from their earliest years. Many experts and viewers have felt the nation has been captured by television documentaries, "soaps," dramas, and situation comedies.

One result of the overexposure to television to which many people have been subjected has been boredom. As a consequence, a smaller number of people watch it.

Second, national concern has been expressed about the kinds of shows that are being broadcast.

Third, television and recorded music have been combined. People under forty seem to have become so used to television images of performers that they expect them to be part of every other form of entertainment.

The need to deal constructively with television viewing has been so great that various ways for families to control viewing habits have developed. One way is to limit the number of hours children can watch TV and to monitor the kinds of programs they watch to make certain violence and immorality are minimal. When unwholesome programs are aired, parents are advised that children should not be allowed to watch. The code of ethics that has resulted will affect the quality and type of programs that will be broadcast into homes in the future.

Video Games

The next assault, in terms of the amount of time they take from the family, has been video games. A product of computer technology, these sophisticated games require skill and coordination. In addition to being exciting, they are attractive and located in places young people frequent. Some restaurants use them as babysitting or time-killing devices for people waiting to be seated or served.

One significant drawback to these games is that they cost money. In order to play the games, young people earn or steal money or wheedle it from their parents. The sums some young persons spend have reached double digits per day. That's a lot of quarters! The situation with video games has become so serious in some communities that they have begun monitoring the arcades in which the games are located. Parents in some communities have insisted that there be a ban on video game arcades and a limit to the number of machines allowed in any commercial establishment.

As with television, pressures brought to the family by video games have been handled by legal means, as well as through attention in the media. The effect of widespread exposure and discussion of a problem generates guidelines that parents can impose on young people. Of course, not all parents control the behavior of their children, nor are all parents interested in monitoring their activities. Nevertheless, the problem has been identified and an atmosphere created in which younger children are not allowed to play video games.

Video games and television are external pressures in the sense that they are products someone else has made. There is not a lot of personal identity or investment at stake either in watching television or playing video games. They are both packaged in such a way that authorities and family groups can control them.

The Personal Computer

The third electronic marvel, the personal computer, has produced an internal, as opposed to an external, strain on families. To be sure, it is packaged and sold like a television set. But the computer requires much more personal involvement than do television and video games. The result of interaction with a computer is more personally rewarding. A family may purchase and use a personal computer, or a corporation may purchase one and an employee may use it at home. It is the very presence of the computer in a home that often causes tension.

Youngsters have to leave the house and get money to play video games, so families can easily impose limits on them. But a computer in the den, basement, or bedroom is readily accessible and harder, therefore, to control. Youngsters do not have to leave the house to use it. They do not need money to play games with it. And the fact that using the computer is socially acceptable, especially if it results in more money for family use, hinders the desire to place limits on its use. The user's age makes no difference. An article in the June 7, 1983, *USA Today* related the experiences of several teen-agers who used their computers to make a fair amount of money. They became models for adults and other teens who have access to a personal computer.

The family with a personal computer is beset by both external and internal pressures. From the outsider's point of view, encouraging family members to use the computer is a good thing. People envy those who own one. A computer might be a step in developing a new career. Such positive reenforcement of a possible obsession with a computer makes it difficult, if not impossible, for a family to establish punitive rules that limit the amount of time a family member spends using the family's computer.

Families nevertheless need some guidance on how to regulate the amount of time each of their members can use the computer. The idea that a son or daughter might become a computer genius who might strike it rich with a new game or program makes some parents far more indulgent than they might normally be. Using the computer seems harmless enough, and many parents would opt for such an activity rather than some of the other activities their young people could get involved with.

Each family, ultimately, has to decide how much time its members may be allowed to spend with the computer. However, we can raise societal concern if we establish an ethical code that addresses the issue of a computer's interference with normal human relationships. Society, through a code of ethics, can assist a family in setting limits if it recognizes that a problem with computer use within families can exist. Our society cannot continue to condone unlimited computer use in families.

The fifth ground rule in developing a computer ethic, therefore, is the need to help families establish rules for use of their personal computers, no matter whether the computer is used for domestic purposes, work, or pleasure. The general social attitude that encourages the computer craze must be replaced by a perspective that insists that families and other intimate groups treat the computer like any other electronic gadget. It should not be allowed to rule people's lives or take away important aspects of family life such as social interaction, the sharing of common experiences, and relaxation together. The computer must be understood as a threat, just as video games and television are threats. Without proper use, they all are detrimental to the family. Used with common sense and governed by reasonable rules, computers can help a family.

Laws As Minimum Protection

A study of business ethics reported in the *Harvard Business Review* in 1977 indicates that legislation is an important method of influencing business practices, but that an ethical code would have a broader impact on the behavior of executives and corporations. [6] The study implied that laws can regulate behavior, but ethics informs and improves it. Although the study does not define ethics, it assumes that those who responded have some clear concepts of right and wrong. The study tended to focus on the "gray areas" of conduct and seemed to assume that ethics reflect a higher form of behavior than obedience to laws, since some of the questions dealt with the ethical dilemma of disobeying laws to benefit the corporation.

Laws provide a minimum amount of protection to a maximum number of people. They are not designed to care for every exception, as court cases that test the limits of most laws attest. Legal minimums are never acceptable to everyone, but they are regarded as a basic standard of conduct or protection in a democratic society. An illustration of the law as setting a minimum standard is the requirement that cars have seat belts rather than air bag restraints. Seat belts are more effective than no safety device at all, but they do not give the consumer the degree of protection an air bag would afford. Tests show that air bags curtail death and injury better than do seat belts.

When laws are enacted, they are intended to describe a conduct code that can be applied to most people in a population. The law seeks to ensure basic levels of behavior. A littering law with a $50.00 fine does not stop some people from littering, but others think twice before they throw their cans and trash onto the roadside. Speed laws are posted to be ignored, according to some drivers, but when the police monitor the speed, these same drivers are the first to slow down. People can easily break a law, but the presence of a law indicates that a minimum level of behavior is expected of all people so that an orderly society can be maintained.

It would be impossible to enact a set of laws that could effectively regulate every possible use of personal computers. There are so many computers in so many different places that have so many uses that the number of laws would become staggering. On the other hand, when we changed from a horse-and-buggy to an automobile society, it became essential to upgrade our laws regarding driving, road conditions, selling and repairing cars, licensing drivers and cars, and policing the highways. A significant change in the type of society we now have will require the same degree of change in our laws.

Most of the laws we will need are already in existence. The difficulty is making the mental and psychological transition from believing that computers are somehow exempt from the law to treating them as another product that must be regulated. There are laws relating to minimum standards for equipment, warranties of products, shoddy sales procedures, repair and replacement of products, and procedures for consumer grievances. These need to be applied to computers.

In addition to these existing laws that can be expanded to apply to computers, there are new areas that need legal attention to protect personal computer users, sellers, and manufacturers. These have to do with such matters as assuring the compatibility of new equipment with existing computers, the interchangeability of devices to hook up computers with printers, and the requirement that retail computer stores give warnings to purchasers of personal computers regarding proper and improper uses of the machine. This group of laws could form a base on which an enforcement policy could be developed. Most of the enforcement would occur at the manufacturering and retail levels.

The sixth ground rule, therefore, for ethics in a computer society is to create a set of laws that can be a minimum level for behavior regarding the use, sales, and manufacture of computers. Additional improvements could be made in the copyright and privacy laws to allow at least some recourse for grievances when an individual's habits or personal information are used without permission by someone having access to a personal computer. The enforcement of any more detailed laws, however, would be diffucult. It is at this point that an emphasis on an ethical code of conduct would be needed.

A Foundation for an Ethical Code

An ethical code seeks to provide information, standards of behavior, and a means for punishing those who ignore or transgress a part of the code. As a first step in developing such a code, ground rules and, within them, areas to be included in the ethics have been defined. The discussion has included: (1) viewing the computer as a tool, not as a substitute person; (2) understanding the capabilities of the computer so many people can use it; (3) paying attention to who controls the computer and its data so people may have access to it and the technician's standardization of society may become a thing of the past; (4) recognizing and protecting people needs for social interaction, stimulation, and relaxation in a computer-dependent society; (5) assisting families to limit the threat of computer overuse by acknowledging that personal computers in the home can be detrimental as well as useful; and (6) the need to develop a set of laws that can provide minimum standards of protection and behavior for computer users, sellers, and manufacturers.

The discussions in this chapter suggest that all parts of society must be involved not only in creating the ethic, but in enforcing it. The long arm of the law is not going to touch most personal computer operators. This limitation on enforcement can allow groups of users of personal computers to develop and send to each other over phone lines pornographic literature, games, and conversations. In addition, limitations on enforcing the law make it possible for computer programs to be developed, advertised, and sold that break the security codes of copyrighted programs. None of these will cease or be hindered until ethical users begin to assist in the enforcement of laws against them.

According to the business people responding to the study reported in the *Harvard Business Review* [7], an ethical code is harder to create and more difficult to support than are laws. The reason is that people are always trying to break ethical codes, and there is no tribunal to which they can be taken. That's the reason it's so important that we, as a society, develop an ethical code that can be subscribed to by those who use the computer, both professionals and nonprofessionals. We are creating a computer-dependent society, and it is our responsibility to insure that the computer is conducive to humane conduct and encourages individual and group social growth. It is time now to turn to a proposed ethical code for the use of computers.

Chapter 5
AN ETHIC FOR A COMPUTER SOCIETY

"How does a computer work?" a college freshmen asked a classmate.

"Fast!" he replied.

"Yeah. But what makes it tick?" she persisted.

"I went to the first class of a computer course once. The instructor gave us a lecture on base 8 and base 10. I was lost in the first five minutes. I never went back. So you're askin' the wrong guy!"

Understanding how a computer works is not essential to using it. But a brief lay description might be helpful. Computers function through an intricate series of electrical impulses. These impulses are generated and controlled in very tiny chips. A program activates the system by telling the computer which impulse is needed at a specific instant. Since so many impulses are involved and because of the computer's speed, you have to write commands for each distinct function, no matter how small.

A good programmer designs a flow chart before writing instructions for a computer. The chart is based on decision points and options the computer is asked to choose between. After the flow chart is precise, programmers write the program so the computer can make decisions that will produce the information they want. Computers are efficient only when the instructions they receive are detailed and specific.

Ethics, which deals with human behavior, is quite the opposite. Ethics, the study of the rules of conduct that apply to individuals and societies, is based on universals rather than specifics. For example, a guide for conduct called The Golden Rule says, "Whatever you wish that men would do to you, do so to them."[1]

This is a universal type of rule since it lets each person decide on specifics. Its intent is to replace the natural selfishness of humans with sensitivity to the needs, hopes, and desires of others.

Immanuel Kant, an eighteenth century German philosopher, believed that the greatest good in human life was possible only when people could live by a set of universal laws of conduct, rather than being swayed by their own or their group's self-interest.[2] Peter Singer, a current philosopher, expands that viewpoint, but he too emphasizes that ethics are based on universals rather than particulars.[3]

Each group, no matter how many or what its origin, develops ethics. For example, each soldering crew in a fabricating department in a steel mill has a set of production and behavior standards by which it expects its members to abide. The standards may be at variance with those established by the company, but the crew obeys its code and not company production quotas. Crew members who break the code by producing too many welds during a shift are told to slow down. If a member persists in overproducing, other members of the crew find ways to sabotage the disobedient crew member's products.

Creating and maintaining a standard of production means that a soldering crew has averaged out the fastest and slowest member's production and, on the basis of these figures, has settled on a range that can include, without too much sacrifice on the part of the faster members of the crew, the efforts of the slowest members. If it becomes necessary for a member to overproduce, such as when that person has extra bills, the crew backs work up and the crew member goes on overtime to catch the crew up. Crew members know how the system works and each new member is educated quickly. Their behavior, as a crew, is based on a code they have created. The code is universal because it applies equally to all of them. The group works out exceptions. In other words, they have their ethics.

We might not agree with the way this particular crew set behavior standards but its example illustrates what is meant by ethics. In the first place, ethics is designed for the good of the group, not for the benefit of an individual or part of a group. Second, everyone in the group is expected to abide by the rules so long as he is a member. Third, individuals are instructed, as soon as they become group members, in the group ethics. The explanation usually includes the rationale behind the ethics and the penalties expected if the code is broken. Fourth, exceptions to the rules are expected, but contingency plans are part of the ethics. Someone—in the previous illustration it was the crew chief—can provide guidance when the code has to be broken. Fifth, the code does not harm the larger society. In this illustration the corporation had a lower production quota than the actual number of solders the crew completed daily.

These, then, are the principles upon which an ethics can be based:

1. Ethics should ensure the good of all members, not a particular group or segment;

2. The code should not allow people to exempt themselves from its precepts because they feel beyond its bounds;

3. The conduct sought by the ethics should be taught to everyone in the society;

4. Exceptions to the rules can be expected, but procedures for bending the codes should be a part of the ethics;

5. Ethics must be enforced to be effective;

6. Conduct codes in one society should not make interaction with other societies or nations harmful or difficult.

Ethics does not exist separately from a legal or social system. Indeed, ethics must be built upon laws. These laws can be statewide or national or international in scope. The discussion in previous chapters stated that laws provide minimal protection—in the case of computers, to purchasers, sellers, and manufacturers.

Ethics is taught, monitored, and enforced by social institutions.[4] The major social institutions entrusted with teaching, monitoring, and enforcing ethics are education, business, government, and religion. Social institutions incorporate ethical codes that can be taught, monitored, and enforced as they deal with their members.

A difficult question, in a large and complex society, is how behavior codes and group norms can be monitored and enforced. A survey of business people regarding ethics[5] suggests that respondents felt their ethics were better than those of others, but they saw no feasible way of forcing others to act the way the respondents did. A discussion of values and norms in a book on technology and the future[6] deals with why an individual decides to abide by ethics, as opposed to being guided solely by self-interest. The conclusion is that an effective ethics depends on a system of rewards and penalties imposed by a majority of the participants in a given society or group. Enforcing a behavior code is dependent upon the collective wills of many individuals. As someone once said, "That's us!"

Given these principles and admonitions, the outline of an ethic for a computer-dependent society is our next concern. The intent of these suggestions is to enable constructive discussion and action that will produce an ethic by which we can live creatively with computers.

Adaptable Standards

1. *Ethical behavior must be adapted to changing situations.*

Customs and approved social behavior change as people construct new environments and fashion new situations. For instance, the marriage contract has become an important part of many marriages during the past decade. Partners want to be clear on relational, custodial, and financial matters prior to their marriage. They want to clarify their specific expectations so that each partner understands the position and feeling of the other. Before they get married, they want to minimize the number of areas for serious disagreement.

The marriage contract is a new situation created by a new environment. The contract idea is not new. What is innovative is that the partners in the marriage are designing the agreement. Historically, contracts have been agreements reached between parents and families of the partners. The partners were pawns and not designers of the contracts. The newness of the situation is that the contract idea is rather widespread and not limited to a few people of a certain region or socio-economic class. The elements of the environment that have helped forge the new situation are af-fluence, the career and work orientation of married women, and an egalitarian attitude regarding women's rights and privileges. Therefore, the socially approved conduct codes of this society vis-à-vis marriage have changed to include the acceptance and usefulness of such contracts.

It is critical that ethical codes, which are a product of a group's thinking, be adaptable to changing social circumstances. A part of the problem with current societal ethics is that they have not ad-justed to deal with issues unique to a computer-dependent society. Until recently, computers were under the jurisdiction of a few pro-fessionals, and the remainder of society was affected primarily through their financial transactions and work. The computer pro-fessionals, it was felt, would develop their own code of ethics, very much as the medical profession constructed its ethical code.

Things changed drastically with the introduction of the per-sonal computer in the late 1970s. No longer are computer data banks under the absolute control of professionals. The computer is available to many people. The ethics of professionals, which were not accepted until 1982, nearly thirty years after the first commer-cial use of computers, are different in substance and intent from those the general populace needs. Professionals work for corpora-tions, but many personal computer users do not. Professionals are governed through their corporations on issues of confidentiality and copyright, whereas many personal computer users do not feel the same restrictions.

The *current ethical code must be adaptable in three ways:* (1) the ethic constructed must be expandable to include any new skills personal computers will be used for, (2) the ethic has to include the possibility that machines will control people, and (3) the ethic will need to include the creation of machines with human-like in-telligence. When these things do come about, people must be pro-tected from control, especially mind control. Ethics must ensure that people retain freedom of choice and maintain control over their life decisions.

The need for ethical adaptability does not mean rules are as changeable as the weather. Codes of conduct change slowly. New ideas are suggested, behavior is tested, and, after a period of time, adjustments to the existing codes are made. Such changes may take a decade or more before they are in place. Partners living together without marriage developed an ethic, but it took several years and was formalized only through a court case. Changes in social concepts come slowly in order to protect the investment most people have in older rules. Just because something is new doesn't mean it's going to last. People must test its durability before they make changes in conduct rules.

The personal computer has been around for several years. Companies and society are convinced it's going to be a staple in the future. Our ethic must be adaptable to probable changes in future technology including: (1) increased amounts of data storage, (2) much quicker access to data banks, and (3) difficulties with preventing unauthorized access to information. Improvements in hardware and software will challenge the ethics, but the challenge will have to be met. So long as we live in a computer-dependent society, we must have an ethics that can deal with whatever advancement society makes in its technology.

The Newly Deprived

Every change in the economics or structure of a society creates a new group of people who are deprived. Affluence results in a deprived poverty group. Large conglomerates have as their counterpoint small, struggling businesses. And an information-glutted segment of society creates an opposite group that is information starved.

There are two sides to every situation. The aspect of the computer-dependent society most often described is its benefits.

There is another side, however. An ethic, in addition to being adaptable, ought to find ways to assist the deprived created by a computer society.

"The Great Society" of the 1960s was heralded as *the* way to eliminate poverty in this nation. Two decades later, poverty and hunger are still with us. It appears that societies, no matter how they are governed or what their dominate philosophy happens to be, separate people into the "haves" and "have nots." Differences in economic opportunities are important. As we move more deeply into a computer-dependent society, a distinction must be made that may be more critical than any economic disadvantage. This is the compounded problem of computer illiteracy and the inaccessibility of computers to large groups of people.

Much previous discussion has dealt with the control of data in computers. It is a part of deprivation. As such, it needs attention first.

2. *The ethic that monitors control of data states that individuals have:*

(1) the right to information, especially about themselves, but also data important to their work and profession;

(2) the opportunity to examine and make corrections when information is inaccurate;

(3) to authorize or deny the use of their personal data by corporations and others; and

(4) no right to unauthorized access to the data stored in any computer.

With an increase in the number of personal computers on managers' desks in corporations, access to heretofore protected data without anyone's knowledge is a likelihood. Therefore, the ethic has to detail behavior and use codes that are beneficial to people.

3. In addition to protecting us from those controlling computers, the *ethic must creatively face the fact that there will be groups of people who cannot use and will not have access to a computer.*

On May 26, 1983, *The Wall Street Journal* in a first-page story described some of the difficulties facing schools concerning computers. A contrast was made between two high schools, one affluent, the other from an inner-city neighborhood. Three differences emerged in the story: (1) a disparity in the number of computers available to the two student populations, (2) differences in the uses made of computers, and (3) wide variations in pupil access to computers at other than school hours. As might be expected, the affluent young people had more computers available in their school, their computers were used as tools to enhance creativity, and several of them had computers at home. This was in sharp contrast to the inner-city school, in which only a few computers were available, the primary use of computers was to train students for word processing and office-type skills, and no one had a computer at home.

This article identifies the new class of deprived. They don't have access to information, nor do they have the facilities that could give them equality. Libraries in some communities, recognizing an obligation to help equalize information access, have begun purchasing personal computers and making them available to residents.[7] Even so, the amount of time an individual can use a public machine is limited. A disparity exists; it can grow to mammoth proportions. This could become a critical society problem in the near future.

As with most distribution issues of society, equality of computer access is a goal. There appears to be only a slight chance of equalizing computer opportunities among public school students, even though schools are often beneficiaries of free computers.[8] In addition, having an opportunity to use a computer at school is not a lasting solution to the problem. Frequency of access is the main difficulty. Individuals who don't know how to use a computer, or those who don't have a computer handy in order to tap into data bases, will be the new deprived groups.

The extent of the information-deprivation issue is evident in the test conducted in our town this past year. Its purpose was to determine the frequency with which a family would use computers if given the opportunity. The companies doing the tests selected 200 homes into which computers and special television sets were placed. The test families could shop, do their banking, tap into data bases, and the like with their computers. Interviews with a couple of the participants found an enthusiasm for computer living. The important part of the test was that this community was selected because it had income, education, and lifestyle patterns that suggested that the residents might be good market potential for the testing company's products. The testers did not conduct their experiment in a low-income, inner-city area because it was obvious that residents there wouldn't be able to pay a high monthly fee to subscribe to the eventual services. Economics will have a significant impact on creating the new deprived class.

In an information society, the people who can secure and use information will be successful, and those who can't get to it or use it will be unsuccessful. The unsuccessful will have little money and not be either able to use or have access to computers. They will not have a computer in their homes to assist their young people with library research, tap into buying services that could help them secure products less expensively than is possible at local stores, or have the opportunity to use the computer to locate appropriate job markets as they search for new positions. This class of under-privileged may be more difficult to deal with than those whose problems are purely economic.

Redistribution of wealth can be legislated if a government and its people are willing. So far neither has been serious in changing the wealth patterns in this society.

Computer literacy will not be easily legislated either. It is assumed that the public education system will take on the task of teaching computer literacy and use. It can provide computers for student use, but, unlike books, computers are not available to carry home. Making the entire population computer literate and able to take advantage of the various sources of information that can aid them in living is an ethical as well as educational task. Providing people *equal access to computers* is an ethical and economical task the logistics of which have not been adequately explored.

This leaves us with a sad fact. An ethic designed for a computer-dependent society will be incomplete. We can make it adaptable to new technology, but we are not farsighted enough to make it so comprehensive that it will include all segments of society because everyone will not have access to the computer. No matter how much we try, there will be a gap between people based on access to and use of information. It is true that an ethic is a beginning point for moving beyond inaction and that it is a plan for creating a tomorrow in which people, rather than machines, will control a society. However, it must do more about attempting to equalize opportunities of access to computers within our society.

Legal Standards

An orderly society is based on laws. A responsible society is composed of people who recognize the rights and privileges of others and are willing to seek the means whereby individuals and groups can work together in harmony.[9] An orderly society composed of responsible people is required before a system of ethics can be created that can inform and guide their behavior toward one another.

4. *An ethical code for a computer dependent society builds upon laws that already exist.*

Ethics is not created in a vacuum, it is the superstructure of a legal system. Ethics represents the expected behavior that supports laws. Since ethics must adapt, it is a certainity that laws must be adjusted. Consumer laws that can be adapted to current conditions concerning computers are those that: (1) prohibit the selling of shoddy merchandise, (2) strengthen manufacturers' warranties, and (3) outlaw misleading advertising.

These adaptations are needed immediately, since the computer is new technology to consumers. Potential consumers aren't certain of the computer's power, nor are they acquainted with the kinds of uses they can make of it. They would like to believe what they are told in articles and by salespersons, but they have no standards by which to judge the accuracy of the claims. Eventually they will establish a knowledge level that will equip them to be careful consumers. In the meantime, however, the legal system can adapt to help regulate the industry, especially the personal computer part of it.

In addition to these three merchandising laws are two that speak directly about information. They (a) protect the confidentiality of data corporations and government have stored in computers, and (b) protect copyright holders. In order for these two laws to be more applicable to the burgeoning personal computer industry they must be revised to: (1) restrict the types of data on individuals that can be stored in personal computers without the consent of the individual; (2) give individuals the opportunity to request and require deletion of data that are stored in personal computers; (3) make it illegal to sell computer programs that can break any type of security codes; (4) set severe penalities for those who pirate programs or sell doctored copies of pirated programs to others; and (5) require those who manufacture copyrighted computer programs to provide backup copies of master disks so that pirating is not necessary.

The current law on confidentiality doesn't go far enough. It has to include personal computers and decree that personal confidential data cannot be stored on them. Another adaptation of the law ought to provide an individual with the right to examine and delete data from the files of a personal computer. Individuals can change and delete inaccurate information currently in corporate and government files through a specific legal process. The same kind of procedure should be applicable to data stored in personal computers. These personal computers can be in corporate offices, homes or private offices. It makes no difference where the computer is, it is the data in them that must be protected. The legal remedy is to have an opportunity to destroy the data, change the file, and obtain whatever solution the injured party might require.

Copyright laws have been changed recently. They need to be broadened to include the personal computer. Some reference to computers is made in the law, but it is not extensive enough. One particular concern is the ease with which personal computer programs can be copied. It makes no difference that there is a security code that locks the program. Someone will find a way to break that code. So long as the benefit to breaking the code is greater than the penalty, the code will be the target of personal computer users. Many dollars are at stake for the person copying programs as well as for the creators of the programs. Laws could, however, make breaking computer security codes very unattractive.

In the current situation individuals may work for large corporations and become familiar with several accounting and forecasting programs that could be transferred to personal computers. These individuals could copy those programs and begin businesses at home by purchasing personal computers and using the pirated programs. If they ran into problems with the program during the day when they were at work in the corporation, they could copy the manual as well. The penalties are minimal. The program developer may tell employees that no backup copies or support will be given to those who haven't purchased a system master. Employees can justify copying the manual as a corporate need. Those who have copied a program and have access to the system master so they can make additional copies can feel relatively safe from corporate as well as legal repercussions.

A similar situation exists when a program is created, then copied by another company that adds one or two small items and sells the program as though it was its creation. This is theft, but it doesn't seem to be covered by a steep enough penalty to discourage it. The copyright law needs to be comprehensive and strong enough to discourage these kinds of activities by personal computer users.

One effective restraint to pirating and selling slightly revised copies of programs to others would be severe fines. It takes time, energy, and money to write and market a good computer program. Some software companies spend thousands of dollars developing and testing their programs. They should be allowed an adequate return on their investment. This can't happen when program pirating is such a common practice among personal computer users.

On the other hand, the law could also ease the problem somewhat by setting standards for backup assistance for those who purchase programs. The software business has moved from the homes of the hobbyist and tinkerer to become a profession on which millions of computer owners depend. There is still a place for the one-person software developer, but if that person puts a product on the market, those who buy it should be assured that the program works and will be backed up by assistance from the program developer if the purchaser encounters any problems.

One of the unpleasant surprises software users have is not being able to get a program to work the way it is supposed to. After some frustration, they may call the program developer and ask for help. The individual on the other end of the line can usually provide the help needed, but some of the technicians at software companies assume the caller has little or no intelligence. While laws will not solve poor personnel problems, a legal requirement to provide purchasers who cannot make a program work with assistance or a new program disk would be a beginning for many personal computer users.

In addition to penalties for pirating and the requirement that program developers provide assistance to purchasers, the law could require companies to give a purchaser enough program disks at a reasonable cost so pirating is neither feasible nor attractive. The delicacy of computer disks is not understood by the neophyte user. A software company needs to give at least two copies of a disk to a purchaser and, if the user is a manager in a corporation with multiple personal computers, provide an inexpensive way to supply the corporation with a larger number of disks and manuals. Since there are so many personal computer users, it might be necessary to enact legal guidelines to ensure that this will happen. The alternative is to encourage pirating, especially by corporate executives.

These suggestions represent legal minimums for confidentiality and copyright protection on personal computers. Laws are in effect that could be adapted to more adequately guide personal computer users. The revisions and expansions of these two laws are necessary to correct current and future problems with personal computer use.

The expansion of consumer protection laws does not need to be significant in order to require warranties on computer manufacturers' products, whether the items are hardware or software. Neither should there be much of an issue in adapting laws to deal with the retailers of computer merchandise. Our difficulty in these areas is lack of knowledge and standards regarding computers and hardware. Until there are some industrywide standards, it will be nearly impossible to provide effective safeguards for the public.

The extension of existing laws would provide minimal legal standards in the current situation. The key adaptation is that they apply to personal computer users. A part of the difficulty in making changes will be figuring out how to enforce the laws. Policing personal computer users by spot checks, similar to the process used by the IRS in monitoring federal tax returns, can be an effective means of enforcement. This is not going to cause all illegal activity to cease, nor is it going to remove all confidential data from personal computers. The legal requirement, however, would provide a means whereby individuals who are harmed by personal computer users who access confidential information can find recompense. Once such legal standards are enacted, a more complete ethic about confidentiality could be constructed.

Maintaining Emotional Health

5. *An ethic places limits on the amount of time people spend with the computer.*

It would make good sense to place a warning sticker concerning the danger of overuse on every personal computer that is sold. The warning might read: "Warning: Computer Use May Be Harmful To Your Personal And Social Life." The computer industry may not welcome such a warning, but it would serve a useful purpose. The need for it is implicit in the words of an employee of a large computer manufacturing firm. "I never had a terminal on my desk before the personal computer came out. Now we each have one and it's a temptation to play with it all the time. It's fun, and I can get so much information out of it. I could spend my entire work day with it and forget about everybody in the office." This comment apparently justifies the need for warning labels to be attached to personal computers.

6. *An ethical code should give personal computer purchasers and users suggested guidelines for usage.* That is, it should state what is and is not a proper use of the computer.

Items 5 and 6 are very important since they deal with a person's interaction with a personal computer. The need to monitor time could be met by including a suggested maximum length of time a person should spend working with a computer each day and week.

A list of suggested uses would be specific to the person or group buying the personal computer. For example, if a corporation was the purchaser, the authorized uses for the personal computers of their managers would deny them access to personnel files, financial data on individuals, and use of the computer for personal or home activities such as list keeping. The uses for a small business would include financial information, inventory, personnel data, and the like. Since the data stored in the small business computer would be limited and authority to use it would be for one or two individuals, the use list would be greater than for corporate managers. A list of uses for families or an individual would include mailing lists, home finances, investment data, games, and recipes.

A second part of the list would identify things for which the personal computer should not be used. This would include engaging in illegal acts such as transmitting pornographic pictures or stories, duplicating copyrighted materials, and other activities that violate privacy and copyright laws, and constitute fraud or inappropriate use of the mails. The list would contain addititional exclusions that would be ethical in nature. It might include: monitoring the personal habits of family, friends, associates, or neighbors; storing information that is defamatory or harmful to others; and using a personal computer to send vulgar, profane, or annoying calls by way of a modem to groups and individuals.

Such warnings are helpful because the check lists can guide individuals, no matter whether they use the personal computer while at work or in the home. However, these warnings do not exhaust the concern for emotional health. Emotional health has been discussed as one of the ground rules for ethics. The discussion related to spending too much time with the computer and treating it as a substitute person. These two concerns are major issues in emotional health, and purchasers must be warned about their insidious possibilities.

7. *Manufacturfers, sellers, and trainers are responsibile for warning purchasers about potential problems.*

Three groups can be helpful in cautioning people about potential emotional and social problems related to the personal computer. In introductory manuals that describe their computers and tell the purchaser how to use them, manufacturers can raise the issue of spending too much time with the computer. No one is going to be frightened away from purchasing a computer because the manual says it is so intriguing that individuals and families should set time limits as to the number of hours a person should spend with it each day. Such a suggestion would, in fact, probably be good for sales, since it indicates that the manufacturer has a sense of social responsibility.

A second group of people who could give such advice to purchasers are the sellers of computers. Retailers and wholesalers can talk directly with corporate consumers and suggest that time limits be imposed on family members, individuals, and employees. The reasons for such a limit are the human need to interact with other people and help users maintain a proper perspective on the computer so it doesn't become a substitute for people.

A third group that can suggest limits on the use of computers are trainers and teachers. These individuals are entrusted with computer literacy training for large groups of personal computer users. In this capacity they can note the dangers, as well as the possibilities, of using computers. The one area they often fail to mention is overuse. It would be relatively easy to include in every seminar or course training aimed at safeguarding the emotional health of the computer user.

The aim of all three groups should be to suggest strongly that computer use not become addictive. This, of course, means it should be understood for what it is, a tool, and used for the kinds of things a computer is built for—storage, retrieval, and manipulation of data. "Protecting emotional health" means trying to shelter individuals who might be psychologically damaged by the overuse of the computer. This protection is an essential aspect of a reasonable computer ethics. It involves everyone who owns and operates a personal computer.

Computers Are Means, Not Ends

8. *An ethic requires computer users to understand their machine, to treat it as a machine, and to use it as a tool.*

People are familiar with fads, acts or behavior that sweep the country, usually through young people, and are gone in a matter of weeks or months. Pet rocks, long hair, short skirts, singing groups, and hula hoops have come and gone. When a fad comes, we know it is a fad and will be short lived.

Conversely, when things start out as fads but become practices we know will change our lives, we get a different feeling. The personal computer produces such a feeling. It is not merely a fad, and it is changing our lives.

A car salesperson watched a young man examine one of the used cars on the lot. After a while, he walked over to the young man and nodded. "How're you doing? Find something you like?"

"I'm not sure. This one looks pretty good, but the price seems a little high."

The salesperson smiled. "That price is rock bottom for the car. It has low mileage and was cared for like a child." He leaned toward the young man and lowered his voice. "An older woman owned it and hardly ever drove it. She was afraid it'd get dirty. Besides, she got on an exercise kick and started walking wherever she went."

The prospective buyer looked at the car and then at the sales person. "I'm looking for transportation, not an investment. I want to know if the car runs, if it uses oil, if the transmission is good, how new the tires are, and things like that. If I wanted it as a museum or show piece, I'd be more interested in your story."

The young man's hardheaded talk revealed that he knew how to keep his need for a car in perspective. He wanted it as a means of transportation. The salesman thought the young man was treating the car as an end, however, something to be purchased for itself, not just a means of transportation.

The approach of the salesperson on the used car lot is similar to that used by his counterparts in retail computer stores. They see the computer as an end—and for them it is. They want to sell it. The purchaser of the car recognized the salesperson's ploy. Many people who are in the market for personal computers are not so informed, nor do they know the kinds of questions to ask before they buy. Many are sold computers as ends in themselves and not as means to perform certain functions.

People go into computer stores with some idea of what a computer can do. Salespersons demonstrate its capabilities by programs and games many individuals do not understand and will never use. Unfortunately, the demonstration is captivating. Before customers know what is happening, they have forgotten their needs and been captured by sales talk. There seems to be something magical in the interchange between customers, computers, and salespersons.

9. *An ethic demands that prospective customers be told several times what the computer can do, what it does best, and that it is a machine that is a means to accomplish a particular series of tasks.*

There is a great deal of misinformation or lack of truthfulness in sales talks about computers. A home computer with limited storage cannot perform most of the tasks a sales person *suggests* it can do. A computer with limited storage is useful primarily for games. A computer with more than 50K memory is used mostly by professionals and small businesses. Also, some computers do not have software available to help consumers do the things they want it for. Most people won't spend the time to learn how to write programs; therefore, the availability of software is critical. This needs to be stressed, but often salespersons conveniently omit important data individuals who want to buy a computer need.

It is critical that the media, through articles in newspapers and magazines, become more accurate in their reporting, rather than being so positive toward computers. People need to know about their limitations as well as their capabilities. Also, they need to understand them as tools and know what they have to do to make them useful for their purposes. The media have a unique opportunity to provide this kind of information. Reporting about the computer should be less biased than has been true of many articles that have appeared in periodicals and newspapers.

Penalties

10. *An ethic has a penalty.*

An ethic, like a law, contains a penalty for disobedience. The penalty may be sabotage, as in the illustration of the soldering crew; it may be ostracism, as practiced by some Old Order Mennonites; it may be starting rumors about someone or something; or it can involve force, as in some vigilante activities. Socially responsible behavior is enforced in different ways, but, to be effective, an ethic must have the power to exact meaningful penalties from those who transgress.

Current laws do not seem to recognize the seriousness of crime committed by people with computers. Individuals who uses computers and electonic devices in criminal ways are called high tech thieves or "hackers." They are an emerging breed and will be especially difficult to discover and apprehend before they do a lot of damage. For example, *The Wall Street Journal* on July 20, 1983 (page 29), printed an article entitled "States Using Computers to Battle Growing Thefts of Jobless Benefits". Employers said they had more employees than were actually working for them. They then used false credentials to make jobless claims benefits for nonexistent employees. The creation of computer profiles that could be used to search for claims was the undoing of several of these would-be thieves.

A report in *USA Today* (page 3A) on July 20, 1983, told about some Indiana prisoners who stole computer codes for the jail telephones and charged more than $1,100 worth of calls and $3,000 in money orders to the prison.

Research Institute Recommendations on May 13, 1983 (page 3), reported that thieves are stealing numbers from credit cards and bank statements. These are computer-access numbers that allow a person to charge items or withdraw money. The high tech thieves working in this fashion steal about one billion dollars a year.

Electronic sophistication does not lessen the likelihood of crime; it increases it. The movie "War Games," while not dealing with crime per se, is an indication of what individuals who are testing out their personal computer can do. When criminals discover the extent of the personal computer's power, no one's finances or privacy will be safe. This is not a promise for the future; it is a reality now. Opportunities beckon to criminals, especially if they have anything to do with the computer.

11. *The ethic requires stronger surveillance and better security for computer systems, no matter what type of computer is involved.*

The July, 1983, issue of *Computer* magazine devoted its contents to computer security technology, or how to create safeguards strong enough to prevent unauthorized access. The thief is not a concern only of law enforcement agencies. Stealing by computer affects everyone. Each person, therefore, has a responsibility to keep watch and report wrongdoings.

12. *An ethic depends on the members of society to transmit it to others and enforce it.*

Earlier we said that an ethic is built on laws. That's the reason an improvement in and expansion of laws dealing with high tech crime are needed. Until there are laws to act as a base, an ethic tends to be directionless. An effective, enforceable ethic has to be built on a solid foundation.

After laws are enacted, the public then has to assist in enforcing not only the laws but also the ethic. Ethics demands that responsible societal members be committed to reporting crimes, testifying against those who break the laws, and enforcing relevant laws, including laws that apply to computers. The ethic, though based on the laws, will contain more stringent behavior codes, such as those that are suggested in the lists of uses for a personal computer. Individuals will be instructued, when purchasing their computers, when they attend classes to learn about the computer, and through articles in the media, that they need to keep an eye out for the possible misuse of personal computers.

It is the personal computer user who will be least policed, no matter how many laws are written. This means personal computer users must monitor themselves and each other. The computer is too dangerous a tool in the hands of one who has evil intents to ignore that individual's use of it. The well-being of many people may depend on the action of one person. The good accomplished by following an ethic outweighs its inconvenience. "Snitching" on a neighbor or a family member will be required if an ethic is to be enforced. If an ethic that rests on an individual's legitimate use of computers is not endorsed and enforced by everyone, it will not be an operative ethic.

The twelve aspects of a reasonable computer ethics suggested above require development, testing, and use. As we conclude our discussion, we need to consider how we can go about building and maintaining an ethic based on these elements for our computer-dependent society.

Chapter 6
BUILDING AND MAINTAINING AN ETHIC

The ethical code approved by the Professional Data Processing Association is expected to be part of the daily behavior of its members.[1] They agree to the code when they join. This ethic, typical of other such ethical codes, includes a procedure for censuring those who ignore or disregard it. Censuring, detailed in the code, begins with hearings that can lead to reprimands and, depending on the circumstances, can eventuate in expulsion from the association. This censure has very serious consequences when an individual tries to secure another job.

The data processor's code is the product of considerable debate, but it is a model at least one other professional organization might consider. Such codes are not unusual in professional organizations. In fact, ethical behavior is necessary to ensure the integrity of each and every profession.

Personal computer users, on the other hand, do not belong to an organization that requires a particular type of conduct. There are, of course, user groups and associations that purchasers of personal computers are invited to join. Some of the groups appear to have an ethic that is binding on their officers. Such a rudimentary ethic opposes the copying of protected programs and limits the kinds of programs the groups make available to their members. They do not, for example, make pornographic or sexually related programs accessible to their clients.

The user associations, however, do not require members to observe specific behavior standards, nor do they seem to be particularly interested in discussing ethics. Their primary concern is to teach members how to use the computer and test out new attachments (peripherals), as well as the new software available for it. Given these interests, it is difficult to ascertain what kind of censure such groups could apply, even if they had an ethic to guide the behavior of their members.

Though there is an apparent lack of concern for imposing ethical standards on user groups, no new organization whose purpose is to create a computer ethic is needed. Ethics for a computer society are extensions of current social mores. That means existing groups need to update their standards. Instead of a new organization, therefore, most organizations should adapt some of their existing behavior codes and policies to the special circumstances concerning personal computers. A 1977 Presidential Study Commission proposed some adaptations to current practices in several groups of organizations with regard to confidentiality.[2]

Essential to the formation of a new ethic is the recognition by computer-related organizations that they ought to assist people to assume responsibility for meeting the unique ethical challenges of a personal-computer-dependent society. Business, government, education, and religion also need, in the near future, to understand the dynamic changes that personal computers are initiating.

The task of these institutions is innovative. Historically, they have been charged with forming behavior patterns and maintaining orderly and responsible social groups. As they participate in forging a computer ethic, they will have to come up with original adaptations of existing social ethics to a computer-dependent society.

Building an ethic does not demand that we start *de novo*. The framework for ethical behavior is available in the form of unwritten dos and don'ts in every group. These unwritten expectations are conveyed to the uninitiated either in informal conversation or through a parent's correction. Breaking an accepted taboo may be embarrassing to the transgressor. When an unwritten code is broken, however, fellow employees or group members are quick to let the person know he has done something he shouldn't do. These unwritten codes of conduct are the framework upon which an ethic for a computer society can be built.

A few examples of such unwritten conduct codes are: "You don't "nark" (tell on) people, especially the members of your group"; "You don't take credit for someone else's work or idea"; "Hurting fellow employees or group members is not acceptable";

"'Showboating' (overproducing, trying to be the center of attention, etc.) is a good way to become unpopular"; "Criticising the way people dress is to insult their taste." These codes are observed strictly by many groups. The rules are conveyed informally and accepted almost universally. When rules are broken, the individual in the group is not respected or is ostracized. The ethics that these statements represent is seen as "common courtesy" by the group. Members would not generally regard them as ethics. However, if they are violated, the group finds ways to punish the offender.

In addition to common group standards, other codes exist that are more demanding. For example, the medical and legal professions have behavior requirements for their members that deal specifically with conduct as a practitioner. Religious groups make ethical demands that cut across professions, work groups, and the social activities of their members.

In short, there are several frameworks upon which the ethics suggested for the computer-dependent society can be built. In the following discussion, the institutions that incorporate some of the prevalent moral codes are identified and suggestions are given for the adaptations needed to change current social ethics to those useful for a computer society.

Responsibilities for Building an Ethic

Recently, a couple of social researchers were discussing the state of the society. Their conversation sounded like this:

"Predicting trends is a lot more risky today than it was a decade ago. It seems as if we no longer have any solid direction," one researcher in his forties said.

"Statistics give some pretty good leads as to what to expect, George. Divorce is up, the number of children is down, jobs are changing, educational attainment is going up, and women are inching their way toward more equality. Those are trends that can be supported by data!" a tall, bespectacled researcher, also in her forties, replied.

"I know that, Stella. Somehow, though, I get the feeling that statistics aren't the best indicator of our national mood. What I'm talking about, I guess, is a lack of a base of beliefs or behavior. Behavior is the better word, I guess. There doesn't seem to be a direction, and that skews the statistics," George said.

"Feelings are pretty soft data, though. You can't make predictions on them. But I appreciate what you're saying. I've noticed it too. Before we can predict with any certainty, we need a moral base in this country. After all, our morals will determine our divorce rate, whether we have more or fewer children, the rapidity with which injustice to women and minorities are addressed, and most everything else in society. Hmmm. Yeah, I know what you mean, George. We don't have a base for anticipating the future."

These researchers were not gloom mongers. They were respected and influential in their field. The concern they probed was not unique to them; it is a favorite topic of social commentators and researchers. A society is dependent on its moral code to determine its future. Some of us might disagree with this conclusion, but it is borne out by most social analyses.[3]

The moral code is the same thing as a group's or society's ethics. Acceptable group behavior generally determines the practices of that society. When there are significant changes in a group's life, the ethics have to be adapted. One such change occurred when the personal computer was invented and became a commercial product bought and used by millions. We discussed some of the changes in earlier chapters.

It is the task of the basic institutions of society—business, government, education, and religion—to inform, monitor, and enforce ethics. Or, to put it another way, the responsibility for informing, monitoring, and enforcing an ethic for a computer society rests with commercial groups concerned with production and exchange; government, which regulates, provides community services, and enforces regulations; education, which instructs the population in behavior and activities acceptable to the society; and religion, which provides a system of beliefs and seeks a good that can raise people from the level of a "dog-eat-dog" existence to a more loving and tolerant social level. Local, regional, state, and national governments regulate and provide services to the population, and enforce their regulations.

In the same way, private and public schools, be they elementary, secondary, trade school, or college, do the instructing for the society. An orderly society depends on these and other institutions to perform their tasks well.

Each institution in the community must build its part of an ethic for a computer society. For instance, business must decide how the society's general ethical behavior applies to manufacturers, sales people, and merchants. The code of ethics to which businesses generally subscribe[4] needs to be adapted. Society, while depending on the business community to lead in making changes in the economic sphere, is not surprised that business is not willing or able to get its members to accept the needed changes. In some ways, in fact, the business enterprise demands an ethic that is at variance with the common good. The struggle for business survival tends to produce ethical nearsightedness in entrepreneurs and managers. In the long run, however, society will hold business accountable either ethically or legally — or both — for an acceptable behavior code applicable to its institutions.

While a single institution cannot create, inform, and enforce an ethic by itself, the institution from which the most is expected in the way of ethics is religion. Churches and synagogues with their rather comprehensive behavior demands can, and often do, inform the ethics of the total society. Churches and synagogues influence all other realms of society. Therefore, what they teach is quite important. The reason for this is clear — people from all segments of society attend those churches and synagogues. Since the basic tenets of almost all our religious institutions are similar, we have a common base upon which to build ethical behavior for the computer age.

Religious institutions, through individual churches and synagogues, influence families, individuals, and the other institutions of society. Its members take their religious background into business, education, and government. No other institutions have such a crossover effect. Churches and synagogues must, therefore help the other institutions in society adapt the current ethical base to a computer society.

Indeed, religion is as much involved with the new personal

computer technology as is any other institution. Churches and synagogues use personal computers and have many members who use them at work and at home. It therefore becomes obvious that any ethical norms adopted and proclaimed by religious institutions can change the way we think about computers quickly and completely.

In addition to using computers, churches and synagogues influence groups in society that are concerned with human caring, such as the family and other support and self-help clusters. The tenets of a revised social ethic can be spread quickly if religious institutions understand the need, accepts their role in creating such an ethic, and use their influence to do so.

Developing an ethic is not the sole task of religious institutions, of course. It also needs the input of business, education, and government, because each of these institutions has a unique role in informing and regulating the people affected by and involved in a computer society. An examination of some of the specific roles of each institution will give a better perspective on how a social ethic is maintained in a complex society.

1. Business. The business community, for example, can develop rules for the proper managerial use of personal computers. In addition to upholding laws on confidentiality and copyright, businesses need to protect individuals and corporations from unauthorized use of personal computers by managers. Corporate rules regarding personal computer use may state that no manager can: (1) access the personnel records of any individual without that person's written consent, (2) divulge or use any information considered privileged but which can be secured through a computer, (3) store or manipulate financial data on individuals or corporations that can be used in ways that can harm them, or (4) take credit for documents to which they have access but which are not their own creation.

Such rules could have a significant impact on the types of activities managers engage in through the personal computer. If such rules could be adopted, they would allow the business community to address, at the outset of the burgeoning use of personal computers in corporations, issues critical to an ethical code.

Establishing rules, either as company policy or in a less formal manner, will not assure their acceptance by every manager, of course. That is too much to hope for! Businesses will be required to enforce the rules in order to protect themselves as corporations as well as their employees and customers or clients. A very important message to business now is that the personal computer can be a powerful tool for evil when its use is unregulated. Self-interest, as well as the greater good of business, demands that corporations and other business enterprises seek to prevent its misuse.

2. Education. Schools are training the people who will eventually become members of the adult population. They are at ages when ethical behavior is being learned. Until now, the basic interest of the schools as far as computers are concerned has been to create a computer-literate student body. They have focused on the teaching of programming skills and individualized learning. They have neglected the more important task of using computers in a responsible way. They dare not be negligent any longer!

Education has the unique responsibility of creating an ethic by example. Not only that, it can enforce its ethic among the learners. A few of the rules and examples it could teach are: 1. Copying programs created by someone else is stealing; 2. The computer should be treated in the same way as any other instrument of learning; 3. Everyone who develops a program, be it a game or software of a functional nature, should not plan to sell it; 4. Computers are more powerful and more destructive than any weapon the operator will ever use, so they should be treated as potentially harmful devices; 5. Social interaction is as important as knowledge and use of a computer; and 6. Experimenting with the computer to break security codes is an invasion of private property and is, therefore, a crime.

Schools need to be involved with computer instructors to establish such rules. These rules are the basis of computer ethics. When put into the hands of young people, computers can do much good or a significant amount of damage. The educational system, as it trains young people, has the responsibility to teach them an ethic and to demonstrate its usefulness by requiring the instructors to abide by it themselves.

3. Government. The basic function of government is regulation, enforcement, and acting on behalf of the larger public. This is done by making and adapting laws, establishing and empowering regulative agencies, and setting up an effective enforcement mechanism. The report of the Privacy Protection Study Commission[5] identifies many ways in which laws and practices can be improved to deal more effectively with an information society. These laws and practices cover the gamut of activities that involve individuals and their personal data.

The difficulty with government is that it must wait for the identification of a problem, study the extent to which the problem affects the public good, debate possible solutions, and become specific with regards to acts before any law can be enacted. The rapidly developing computer society can't wait for such machinery to slowly grind into action. An ethic must be in place to guide its members so government can take its time in deliberative action without injuring segments of society.

As Willis H. Ware has noted, technology is growing faster than government can respond.[6] The activities of a computer group from Milwaukee in August, 1983, points out the gaps in laws. They accessed confidential and secured data records just to see if it was possible. There are no laws that directly apply to them. The government, therefore, needs to carefully consider how to legislate protection and penalties for such cases in the future. Meanwhile, it is up to the other institutions in society to regulate computer users by a more formidable ethic.

4. Religion. The religious institution is the one we expect to establish and maintain an ethic. Religious institutions are deeply rooted in the past and have a tendency to be a generation behind in creating behavior models. In this respect, they are important conserving institutions. However, they need to be in the forefront of a social change as significant as the one produced by the advent of the computer. Unless religious institutions develop a strong ethic, other institutions will have limited guidelines for the creation of their ethic.

Maintaining An Ethic

Maintaining an ethic, after it is developed, is done through information, monitoring, and the assessment of penalties to those disregarding the code. The illustration of the welding crew in chapter 5 indicates how an ethic is maintained. It is kept in place because group members feel a responsibility for upholding it. They feel this responsibility because they are among those people who are confronting similar obstacles and have work goals that are similar. The similarity of obstacles and goals is due primarily to some external characteristic. In the case of the work crew, it was their jobs and the personal computers they owned and used that produced the similarities.

In a fundamental sense, adhering to an ethic might seem to be in one's best interest. This is not necessarily true, however. Ethics are based on universal laws or codes that benefit the majority. By definition, therefore, ethical behavior limits the activities of the rest. The reason institutions are given the responsibility for maintaining an ethic is that any rule is not always in the best interests of a specific person.

By the same token, institutions depend upon their members to inform, monitor, and enforce an ethical code. While the business community may endorse an ethic through a trade or commercial association, it relies on the businesses that are part of its membership to inform their employees, to monitor their activities, and to correct the employees when they disobey the guidelines. This kind of dependence may seem to put associations at a disadvantage in trying to maintain an ethic, but it appears to be the only mechanism, other than laws, that is effective.

A hypothetical case can illustrate the manner in which business might uphold an ethic related to personal computers. Let's suppose we are talking about a trade association for personal computer manufacturers and merchants. (Such a combination is unlikely, however, since manufacturing and merchandising are different trades.) The trade association would establish and endorse an ethic related to manufacturing and retailing personal computers. The ethic would: (1) seek to standardize the industry so consumers might be able to interchange or at least compare systems and system components; (2) ask members to establish an effective warranty, service plan, and dealer support system; (3) request manufacturers to make certain that their manuals contained warnings about proper and improper uses of personal computers, possible negative effects of computer overuse, and illegal activities related to copyrights and confidentiality; (4) entreat members to insist on training for every salesperson handling their merchandise, whether that person is selling at the wholesale or retail level; and (5) appeal to members to provide accurate informational literature for potential consumers. These ethical guidelines, after approval by the association, would be sent to each member business for implementation. It would then become the duty of each member, manufacturer, or retailer to abide by them.

This would mean, for instance, that the association would depend on XYZ Corporation to monitor and maintain the ethic among its employees. This may require the corporation to review its policies and adjust them to deal with personal computers in the light of the association's ethical guidelines. It also means that managers would be informed of the guidelines as they are oriented to the use of the personal computer. It would probably include a discussion of ethics as part of each continuing education course offered within the corporation.

When the corporation fails to maintain the ethic, the business community through its trade association would be expected to impose penalties for the corporation's failure. If, within the corporation itself, a manager persisted in breaking the code, it would be the responsibility of the corporation to censure the manager. The need to compose, implement, and enforce an ethic may seem to depend too heavily on voluntary compliance, but that's the nature of an ethic. It is also a major failing. In this illustration the ethic must be broad and strong enough to convince members of the association that it is in their interest to maintain it.

The procedure for establishing and maintaining an ethic in an educational system is just as complex as it is in business. The separate entities are school boards and trustees rather than corporations. As individuals, teachers may develop and practice an ethic, but without a general policy, the ethic is personal practice, nothing more. School boards, like corporations, need to establish binding policies for computer use.

Instructors of a computer class may have an ethical standard that they teach to their students. This standard might cover illegal and improper use of the computer, copying and pirating software, breaking security codes, and abuse of personal time by overusing the computer. These ethical standards might be great, but this instructor may be only one of five or ten in the district who are teaching students about the computer. Other instructors will probably have different standards. In order to develop a uniform ethic, all instructors must teach it. Therefore it has to be a policy of the school board that each instructor is expected to inculcate. In addition to making instructors aware of the ethic, enactment of an ethic by the school board gives administrators the ability to enforce it.

It is very important that young people, who are often "turned on" by the computer, learn the ethic so it will be a useful tool in the future. They need to be taught the ethic so their energies can be channeled into productive rather than destructive experiments with their computers.

Schools are important for the spread effect of the ethic they teach. For example, an ethic taught at school may influence whole families because students may bring it home. It may guide them as they work with the computer. If a parent breaks one of the rules, a son or daughter may then say "Mr. Jones said that isn't a proper use for a computer because . . . ." The parent then at least knows there are bounds within which the young person has been taught to live. In this manner, an ethic regarding computers enacted by the school board influences whole families. Not only that, the ethic may become normative because the students in the family will encourage its enforcement.

This illustrates the spread effect of an ethic. What is taught in one setting does have a bearing on how people use the computer in another situation. This is the overlap or, to use an educational term, reenforcement of learnings, that people must have in order for an ethic to become part of their normal behavior.

The government helps maintain an ethic through its legislative, regulatory, and enforcement activities. It takes considerable time for laws to be enacted but to be most effective, they must be built on existing standards. Ethics, at this point, become almost circular in dependence. Ethics are based on laws, and adaptations to the law encompass changes in existing ethics. Social change happens in this cyclical fashion unless there is a societal disaster. Even though computers have made a significant impact on society, the impact has not been disastrous. Their impact can be accommodated by expanding existing mores.

Rapidity of change can force the government to act more quickly than normal. This may have to be the case with computers. The spread of personal computers and the ability of people to use them has been telescoped into half a decade. Experts thought the information society would come during this century, but not quite so rapidly. Even so, the privacy commission has laid a foundation for considering not only new laws but a procedure and rationale for expanding existing laws to deal with personal computers. In many ways, the groundwork necessary for most of the legislation that must underlie a sound ethic is already in place. This doesn't mean debate will be easy or unspirited. What is meant is that the basics for new laws are ready for additional superstructures.

The religious institution, meanwhile, has been busily experimenting with personal computers. At the congregational level religious leaders and members put mailing and membership lists on personal computers. They have also begun to adapt some of the software created for home use to church and synagogue use. Mostly, after adapting mailing and membership list software, financial record keeping has been done by computer. A goal of these leaders has been to find ways to increase giving by keeping track of people and their interests more accurately. As a result of the separate efforts of personal computer users in many congregations, a considerable array of personal computer expertise is available to religious groups.

This expertise has focused its attention on creating software that can be sold to other congregations. The program developers, as might have been predicted, have concentrated on finance and membership records as well as mailing lists, although some software is available that catalogues religious books. Also, disks with one version of the Bible are available and can be used with a concordance program.

It is evident to any serious observer that the attention of religious leaders has not been on the ethics of computer use. Instead, their four primary concerns seem to be: (1) whether or not a personal computer would be useful to their own congregation; (2) that no one will know how to use a computer effectively even if the congregation got one; (3) that a great deal of effort will be required to raise money to purchase an adequate system; and (4) that they are uncertain which components are essential for a system to be adequate for their congregation's present and future needs. These concerns are further evidence that religious institutions have not gotten around to thinking seriously about the ethical aspects of personal computer use. They are still in the process of looking at, studying, and understanding them.

Religious leaders are not unusual in their slowness to turn their sights beyond embracing a new technology. As with any new technology, curiosity and excitement precede concern. Currently, curiosity reigns. As a side interest, many members of religious groups have experimented by using their computers to assist their local congregation or synagogue. These experiments have created an interest, but for most congregations, buying a computer is still a great leap into the future. As with people, congregations are more interested in taking small steps. Therefore, religious leaders have been content to encourage congregational members to continue to do membership and mailing lists.

A few congregations have gotten into computer use because a member either gave them some hardware or agreed to write the software if the congregation purchased a particular kind of personal computer. Either arrangement allows a congregation to invest in computer technology with limited financial commitment. This procedure works best when an authoritative committee within the congregation approves it.

In those congregations that have begun to use personal computers, a primary concern has been confidentiality, especially when the computer is used to store and update individual giving and pledging records. These figures are tightly guarded by most congregations. Allowing several people access to them through a personal computer has been a serious concern. A solution has been to keep the data disks in the office and allow only one person to care for the records. Of course, this raises the issue of monitoring the record keeper, a trustworthy person in most cases, fortunately.

This discussion indicates that religious institutions have not been thinking seriously about ethics in a computer society because most of them have not been involved with computers very much yet. When it does become interested, however, its major concerns, in addition to confidentiality, will be with computer addiction. Such addiction does not create an environment in which people can focus on their feelings. It limits interaction to a machine. Other concerns will include emphasis on concerns that will produce personal growth, and attempts to strengthen the ethical viewpoint of members whose work activities involve personal computer use. Religious institutions, hopefully, will seek to provide an underlying base upon which other institutions can create a relevant ethic.

Earlier in this book much was said about the computer, some issues surrounding its use, dangers to people who would escape from a human environment by isolating themselves with a personal computer, ground rules for an ethic, and building and maintaining an ethic. It is appropriate, as a conclusion to this book, to bring these strands together by illustrating how the church and synagogue might go about creating an ethic for a computer society. This illustration can be used as a point of departure for the other major social institutions as they strive to adapt current social ethics to an emerging computer-dependent society.

A Religious Ethic for a Computer Society

The primary interest of the religious institution is human life and interaction. In terms of the twelve items of ethics listed in chapter 5, this means numbers 2, 3, 4, 5, 6, 7, 8, and 11. While the other items need to be dealt with, these are the primary concerns of religious institutions. Each of them has to do with users or people affected by personal computers.

1. Care for People. A cardinal matter regarding computers is to emphasize the human approach and attitude in society. The categorization of people, ideas, and things because of the computer has occurred rapidly during the past three decades. We have been under the rule of technicians. The religious institution has acquiesed to this rule because it smacked of "progress." It hasn't, in fact, been progress so much as it has been regimentation.

In not protesting the methods and long-range implications of fixed standards, religious institutions have neglected their obligation to monitor computer activity from the point of view of a concern for people. It may be that arranging people into groups with the "average," a statistical straw person, being the most acceptable pattern is the best way for a complex society to handle its affairs. Somehow, though, this doesn't fit with religious beliefs, which elevate persons to become communicants with God.

The long-term implication of the statistical average is to exclude any kind of encouragement for the deviant, including the above average individual, who might want to change the system. Society has managed to find ways in the past to encourage positive deviancy, even though the result has been to change social history. Indeed, history shows that the religious institution often has been a champion of the deviant. (History records as well, however, numerous instances in which religion has severely punished and forcibly forbade any deviance.) In this computer age, however, the church and synagogue have been silent. Their ethics have been wound up in international affairs to the point that their attention has been diverted from more dangerous enemies within the society.

As the religious institution begins to consider adapting ethics to a computer oriented society, it must start with monitoring the society in order to assure that people are treated as people and not herded into bins convenient for processing by computers. This is not a new problem, but the religious institution has yet to meaningfully address it from the point of view of caring for humans. This will become a much more critical issue in the future unless machines are designed in such a way as to empower individual creativity and discontinue the emphasis upon the average.

Averages are fine when comparing batting scores or football

yardage. However, when a person's potential is compared to the most frequent achievement of others of the same age or grade, the concept of average can be demeaning. Psychologists and religionists alike say that humans have not begun to touch the potential of their capabilities. Yet, when the average is looked on as the Golden Rule of achievement, motivation to reach one's potential is stifled. An ethic worth talking about will question our reliance upon the "average" and replace it with a much more stimulating and challenging goal.

The need for such an ethic has been stressed throughout the discussions in this book. Our technology-dependent society must find ways to rise above the rigid demands of the computer. It is up to the religious institution to keep this need directly before the entire society. We must stop being so enamored with machinery and become more interested in caring for people.

2. Create An Environment For Feelings. "I worked nearly 12 hours yesterday, and it looks as though I might be here at least that many today. Just think of the money I'm going to have in my next paycheck!" Diane exulted.

"More power to you, but I'd just as soon be around to spend what I earn. If you work so many hours, when do you have any left to do other things?" Harriet retorted.

"What other things?" Diane asked.

"You've answered my question," Harriet quickly fired back.

Part of a computer ethic will include limitations on the amount of time spent on personal computers. The work ethic has been cited often as the underlying philosophy upon which the industrial dominance of the U. S. A. by the mid-twentieth century has been based. The work ethic is advocated even now by many corporate managers. That's one aspect of the problem with a computer-centered society. People don't know when to quit! They become isolates. They disrupt family life through addiction to the computer. And they would rather watch words run across a video screen than listen to them from the mouth of a friend or companion. An ethic must help them become human once more.

In addition, unions will hopefully lead the fight against computer domination of employees. This will involve negotiations and legal battles around the issues of piece work and unfair labor practices when all work is clocked by averages computed by machines. It will also involve the provision of benefits to homebound workers. In each of these areas, unions will be seeking to guarantee employees the opportunity to be treated as human beings who need to interact with other human beings, and to rest. In a computer-dependent society, corporations and businesses of all sizes can be tempted to program machines to monitor and evaluate employees. This procedure will turn people into robots.

Religious institutions will need to support union efforts to maintain humane environments in which people can be productive. They will insist, as well, that employees be granted time to be creative, rest, and interact with other people. A computer-dependent society may make interpersonal relationships far more intermittent than has been true in the past. The opportunity to get to know others will be severely limited because of the computer bins in which many, if not most, people will work.

Religious institutions have the unique privilege—and obligation—to create environments in which people can cultivate and share feelings and emotions. They should be concerned with the growth and development of human beings. Religious institutions have a lot of experience in creating and maintaining feeling environments.

The contribution of the religious institution to an ethic for a computer society can be to retain and expand its abilities to help people generate and renew feelings and share emotions. When this is combined with an attitude of care, individuals will be better able to handle some of the difficulties associated with life in a computer society.

3. Training People to Grow. No matter how hard religious institutions try to care for people and create environments in which the emphasis is on feelings, they cannot do so without at the same time getting people to see the need for personal growth. It becomes a much more serious responsibility in a computer society, therefore, to train people to share and to interact with issues of deep human significance so personal growth will occur.

A family we know recently entertained relatives and friends

from another part of the nation. The visitors had a limited range of experience and little exposure to the diversity of people and ideas that exist in our country. The host family gave the visitors a few tours and introduced them to some places in which individuals with unfamiliar ideas, dress, and customs lived and worked. It was an eye-opening and mind stretching time for the visitors. As they departed, one of them said, "This has been a mind boggling visit. I never knew there were so many different kinds of people in the world. Thanks for the education!"

The major social institutions can help people from different cultures and backgrounds become acquainted with each other and share different ideas. Religious institutions, however, can do this as part of their program. That's why they are the best at working with such issues as poverty, prejudice, and justice. They can intentionally train members and advocates to think about and handle issues that cause other social institutions to stumble. In fact, society depends upon religious institutions to fulfill this function.

This isn't to imply that society will thank religious institutions for sensitizing its members to injustice, however. When corrective measures are proposed, religious institutions will encounter the wrath of business, education, and perhaps even government. Nevertheless, unless religious institutions persist in training their people to deal effectively with issues of human significance, such problems will be handled on the basis of biased self-interest and certainly will not have high priority in their lives.

Such training is especially important in a computer society. The danger of being controlled by machines is overshadowed by the danger of thinking like machines. Learning a computer program is like learning to eat once again, only this time it is chewing on tiny bits and bytes. Computer software is dependent upon breaking things into their smallest components. Living, especially when it involves religious beliefs, produces a larger, more holistic view of one's place in all of life. This elevates others and reduces one's own importance. This is a view contrary to the "me first" or "number one" philosophy most often advocated by secular elements in our society.

Religious institutions, with their firm belief in God's care and our need to share love with others, are uniquely qualified to add training in thinking about issues of human significance to an ethic in a computer society. When this is done in an atmosphere that encourages personal growth, i.e., mind stretching experiences, the danger of being controlled by machines is lessened immensely. While some of these concerns would relate to the practical issues of computer use, others might develop a philosophical and moral base for long-term human growth by a creative use of the computer. This would be taking the computer from the technicians and making it a public entity that can respond to human desires.

4. Demonstrate an Ethic. An ethic is esoteric until it is put into practice. We can talk in "musts," "shoulds," and "oughts" from now until the end of time. An ethic for a computer society is not talked into being, it is practiced. Those with the most to lose by an ethic are those gaining the most right now — manufacturers and sellers. They might be disposed to consider an ethic something that others might want to be concerned about but that they can do without.

An attitude such as this is not unusual. Changing behavior patterns is often thought to be the responsibility of someone or something else. This gives to religious institutions a singularly attractive opportunity to develop an ethic that can be copied by the other major social institutions. The components of this ethic will be such that they can be incorporated into any ethic created by the other social institutions.

This ethic would guarantee individual integrity by: 1. keeping a minimum of data about any person in computers; 2. allowing every person an annual opportunity to correct personal data held in any computer; 3. instructing people in the proper and improper uses of a computer; 4. giving each person access to and knowledge of how to use a computer; and 5. providing guidelines for a time allotment for computer use. The religious ethic also would encourage people to use a computer, equalize opportunities for computer use, and discourage misuse of personal information.

In addition the ethic would stress: 1. the privacy of information; 2. the protection of products people create, through an expanded copyright law; 3, the need to understand what the computer can and can't do; 4, the use of a computer as a tool that can relieve drudgery and aid in creativity; and 5. that people make decisions, while computers process data. This ethic would be people-directed and would speak even to religious groups that may have a tendency to exploit volunteers in the realm of computer work.

Concluding Remarks

An ethic for a computer society will not be the product of one person or one social institution. Computer users, sellers, manufacturers, and all those affected by computers will need to interact with the issues that have been identified in this book, plus many other concerns that will emerge in serious discussions. The need is to begin the discussion and set some basic standards right now. This book pleads for just such an immediate start. The standards we have suggested are not unreasonable and can be attained shortly—if we want to accept them. However, before we accept standards, we must engage in the discussion of ethics so that together we may create the right context for a computer-dependent society.

EPILOGUE*

This book represents more than a discussion of computer ethics. It is a breakthrough for the writer and the publisher. We discussed the possibility of my writing being transferred directly from a personal computer to the publisher's typesetting word processor. We decided to do it even though neither of us had done it before.

I had been using a word processing program but knew it was written in a computer language that needed to be translated before it could be transmitted by the modem software I had. Three calls to the software developer convinced me that: (1) the company wasn't interested in assisting me to make any translation; (2) the company had focused its attention on a model of personal computer that I do not own and its support of the program I was using was less than casual; and (3) it would be best for me to purchase a new program.

As luck would have it, a friend gave me some data about a different program in mid-June. A new version was being introduced that worked on my computer and appeared to be just what was needed. In addition, it was being sold as a promotional item at a discount.

It takes time to learn how to use a computer program. Surprisingly, this program was easy to get acquainted with, probably because it worked much like the one I had been using. Early in August we felt the time had come to try a transmission.

The inability to transmit our material frustrated us, but we went back to the manuals. We had trouble making a connection because we had to go through a switchboard. That was solved when we reversed the calling procedure from my computer to that of the publisher. That wasn't too helpful because I couldn't get the modem to find and send the files. We broke off to do some more homework.

One call to the software developer solved the file problem. The program was written in a DOS that had to be translated to another DOS before it could be transmitted. The procedure was simple, and I had both the instructions and experience to do that. Following a weekend of preparation, we tried to send files again. After being unsuccessful in the connect procedure and then reversing the calling pattern, we sent two files! What a relief! The machines actually worked as they were supposed to!

The manuscript was transmitted in about two and a half hours through the telephone. I sent hard copy for the person working with the word processor to use in cleaning up the text. It was exciting to be able to make such a transmission but emphasized the need for guidelines for computer use. We were guided by an ethical code from a religious background. The ease with which the information was sent and the rapidity with which it became a book are enough to convince us that others with a contrary set of ethics could quickly cause damage to people or corporations in their efforts to transmit copy.

This little machine in front of me has encouraged creativity. Somehow, we who use them and are affected by them need laws to guide us and behavior codes to follow. Otherwise, we can do whatever we want in the information and communication fields. That can't be beneficial to society.

----

*Thanks to John Braden for suggesting that our experience in transmitting our data be part of this book.

NOTES

Chapter 1: Computers Everywhere

1. Peter A. McWilliams, *The Word Processing Book* (Los Angeles: Prelude Press, 1983).
2. Harry Wulfort, *Breakthrough to the Computer Age* (New York: Scribner's, 1982).
3. Alvin Toffler, *The Third Wave* (New York: Bantam Books, 1981).
4. "DPMA Code of Ethics and Standards of Conduct for Information Processing Professionals," *Data Management,* December 1981.
5. George B. Trubow, "Microcomputers: Legal Approaches and Ethical Implications in Computers and Privacy in the Next Decade," in Lance J. Hoffman, ed., *Computers and Privacy in the Next Decade* (New York: Academic Press, 1980).
6. Toffler, *The Third Wave.*

Chapter 2: Putting Personal Data in Your Computer

1. James Martin and Adrian R. D. Norman, *The Computerized Society* (Englewood Cliffs, N.J.: Prentice-Hall, 1970).
2. Steven S. Ross, "Putting Computers to Work," *U.S. Air,* May 1983.

Chapter 3: Decision-Making

1. "The Race for the Supercomputer," *Newsweek,* July 4, 1983.

Chapter 4: Ground Rules for Ethics in a Computer Society

1. See *Data Management,* December 1981.
2. "Stevens Blazing a Trail in Personal Computers," *The New York Times,* May 30, 1983, p. 21.
3. Ashley Montagu and Samuel S. Snyder, *Man and the Computer* (Philadelphia: Auerbach, 1972), p. 152.
4. A. Richard Immel, "The Micro-Mainframe War," *Popular Computing,* June 1983.
5. "'Electronics Holds the Key' to Keeping U.S. Competitive," *U.S. News and World Report,* August 1, 1983.
6. Steven N. Brenner and Earl A. Molander, "Is the Ethics of Business Changing?" *Harvard Business Review,* January-February 1977.
7. *Ibid.,* p. 63.

Chapter 5: An Ethic for a Computer Society

1. Matthew 7:12 *(R.S.V.).*
2. Immanuel Kant, *Fundamental Principles of the Metaphysic of Morals.* Harvard Classics, vol. 32, pp. 305-17.

3. Peter Singer, *Practical Ethics* (New York: Cambridge University Press, 1979).
4. Paul Tillich, *Morality and Beyond* (New York: Harper and Row, 1963), p. 94.
5. *Harvard Business Review,* January-February 1977.
6. Kurt Baier, "What Is Value? An Analysis of the Concept," in Kurt Baier and Nicholas Rescher, eds., *Values and the Future* (New York: The Free Press, 1969), pp. 33-37.
7. "Rural Libraries Offering Time on Microcomputers," *The New York Times,* August 13, 1983, p. 6.
8. "Computers May Widen Gap in School Quality Between Rich and Poor," *The Wall Street Journal,* May 26, 1983, p. 1.
9. Walter G. Muelder, *Foundations of the Responsible Society* (Nashville: Abingdon Press, 1959), p. 23.

Chapter 6: Building and Maintaining an Ethic

1. *Data Management,* December 1981.
2. *Personal Privacy in an Information Society.* The Report of the Privacy Protection Study Commission (Washington: U.S. Government Printing Office, 1977).
3. Robert L. Heilbroner, *The Human Prospect* (New York: W. W. Norton, 1974).
4. *Harvard Business Review,* January-February 1977.
5. *Personal Privacy in an Information Society.*
6. Willis H. Ware, "Privacy and Information Technology — The Years Ahead," in Lance J. Hoffman, ed., *Computers and Privacy in the Next Decade* (New York: Academic Press, 1980).